RICHMOND *Handbooks* **FOR ENGLISH TEACHERS**

Series Editor : Paul Seligson

Teaching
Very Young
Children

Pre-school and
Early Primary

Genevieve Roth

Richmond
PUBLISHING

Richmond Publishing
19 Berghem Mews
Blythe Road
London W14 0HN

ISBN: 84-294-5446-2
Depósito legal: M-15509-1998
Printed in Spain by Palgraphic, S. A.

| **Layout** | Gecko Ltd |
| **Cover Design** | Geoff Sida, Ship Design |

Illustrations   Amy Arnold, Phill Burrows, John Plumb, DTP: Harvey Collins

Author's Acknowledgements
I would like to thank Remei Gomez Martinez, psychologist in Denia, for helping me with Chapter 1, and my son, Daniel J., for teaching me how to use a computer. I would also like to thank all of my children, Rebeka, Daniel J. and Bruno, and especially my husband, Juan, for their encouragement.

Map of the book

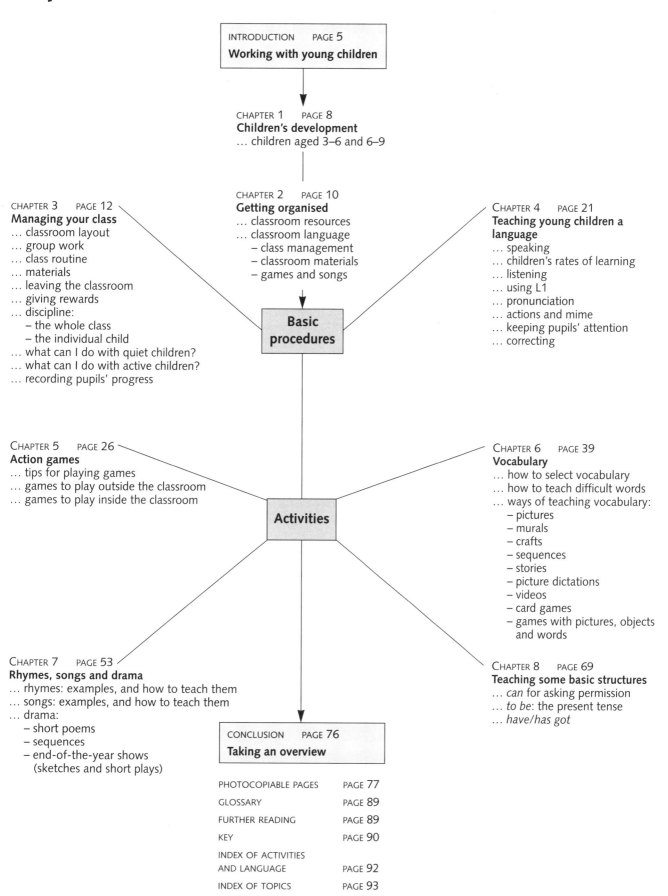

Richmond Handbooks for Teachers: An introduction

This series presents key issues in English Language Teaching today, to help you keep in touch with topics raised in recent educational reforms. The books all contain a mixture of analysis, development work, ideas and photocopiable resources for the classroom. The key note througout is what is **practical, realistic** and **easy to implement**. Our aim is to provide a useful resource which will help you to develop your own teaching and to enjoy it more.

While each of the books has been written for the practising English Language Teacher in the primary or secondary environment, they are also suitable for teachers of languages other than English, as well as for teachers of young adults, trainee teachers and trainers.

All classroom activities are designed for lower-level classes (from beginners to lower intermediate) as these form the majority of classes in both primary and secondary. Most of them can, however, be easily adapted to higher levels.

The books all contain:

- *a section of photocopiable activities and templates*. These are either for immediate classroom use (some with a little adaptation to suit your classes) or for use throughout the year, e.g. in this book, lists of classroom language.

- *regular development tasks*. These ask you to reflect on your teaching in the light of what you have just read, and some ask you to try new ideas in the class. They are all intended to make the ideas in the books more accessible to you as a classroom teacher.

- *an index of activities/topics*. As most teachers dip into or skim through resource books, there is an index at the back of each book to help you find the section or ideas that you wish to read about.

- *a comprehensive glossary*. As one of the main principles of the books is ease of use, the authors have tried not to use jargon or difficult terminology. Where this has been unavoidable, the word/term is in SMALL CAPITALS and is explained in the glossary at the back. Likewise, we have avoided abbreviations in these books; the only one used which is not in current everyday English is L1, i.e. the students' mother tongue.

Although all of the ideas in these books are presented in English, you may need to explain or even try some of them, at least initially, in the students' L1. There is nothing wrong with this: L1 can be a useful, efficient resource, especially for explaining methodology. New ideas, which may challenge the traditional methods of teaching and learning, can be very threatening to both teachers and students. So, especially with lower-level classes, you can make them less threatening by translating them. This is not wasting time in the English class, as these ideas will help the students to learn/study more efficiently and learn more English in the long term.

Working with young children

"Who is this book for?"

This book is designed for teachers who are teaching English as a Foreign Language to children between the ages of three and nine. However, most of the activities can be used with children with a low level of English, up to the age of eleven.

The book is intended for teachers who have little, or no, experience of working with young children and/or teaching English as a Foreign Language, but it may also provide the more experienced teacher with some useful new ideas.

"What will I find in this book?"

As you will see from the Map of the book, the book provides background information on child development, practical information on organising your classroom, advice on basic teaching procedures, and detailed descriptions of activities. The activities aim to teach young children to communicate orally (to understand others' speech and to make themselves understood). This is the only way they communicate in L1 until they are about five (the age a child learns to read and write obviously varies).

Throughout the book, the child is referred to as *he* and the teacher as *she*. This style has been used for the sake of simplicity, and is not intended to exclude either gender from the reader's image of the child or teacher.

"What about reading and writing?"

You cannot expect children to communicate in English in ways that they cannot communicate in their first language. If children are asked to read and write in English when they are not skilled or mature enough, learning to read the language becomes an arduous and unpleasant task. So children should have fairly good oral communication skills in English before they learn how to read and write in English. However, if their hand–eye and spatial coordination are adequately developed, and they understand what they are reading, they will be able to learn to read English quite quickly and with confidence. They will also be able to read aloud with good pronunciation if they can identify the words on the page with language they have already heard. If reading is enjoyable they will feel encouraged to read more, and later to write. If they are able to express themselves, then writing will be a creative rather than a mechanical task.

All the activities included in this book are a useful basis for teaching young children to read and write in English later, and some of them can be adapted into written activities for children who already know the language used in them.

"What is the difference between teaching and educating?"

Teaching a child could be defined as instructing him in a certain area. Educating a child, however, is enabling him to develop mentally, morally, physically and socially, and as such it encompasses teaching. You can teach a child to brush his teeth just like you can train an animal to perform a trick, but to educate him you need to explain the reasons for doing so. You cannot teach something to a very young child without educating him first.

When a three- or four-year-old starts school, he may never have been away from his mother for any length of time, may have had very little contact with children of his own age, or at the most, have had contact with only a very small, secure group. Going to school is an enormous step and the first thing a child has to do is to become socialised in this environment. This means learning:

… the 'dos and don'ts' of getting on with others

… how to be accepted by others and how to accept them

… how to gradually become independent, whilst taking part in a community that is much wider than the family circle.

This part of the child's socialisation is the first step in the child's school education.

It is our responsibility as teachers to help our pupils to develop and mature as well as learn. It is no easy task as we are setting the basis for the years to come. The main things to remember are:

… enjoy your young pupils

… be as relaxed as possible

… be firm and consistent in your discipline.

Physical contact with the teacher

When a three- or four-year-old knows you and is comfortable with you, he usually wants a lot of physical contact. When he arrives in the classroom he may come straight to you and hold onto your leg or stand by your side, waiting for a sign of affection that will make him feel secure before he goes off to play. His dependence on you will be almost total.

Little by little, over the next few years, he separates himself both physically and psychologically from his teachers, becoming a more and more independent person. However, even seven- and eight-year-olds still need direct physical contact with their teacher at times. You will see them find an excuse to sit beside you or fight among themselves to hold your hand when you stand in a circle with them. Provide physical contact simply by placing your hand on a child's shoulders when speaking personally to him or by smacking a palm of your hand against one of his, or by shaking his hand to congratulate him, saying *Good for you!* as you do so.

Teaching children a language

A point of reference
Many children who enter school at the ages of three and four are not yet able to speak their own language properly or clearly. However this does not mean that they cannot learn another language, or even two or three other languages, at the same time. Learning that second or third language is easier for the child if he has a way of keeping the different languages separate. His point of reference could be, for example:

… L1 (his first language) is used with one teacher and English is used with another, or

… L1 is used in the morning and English in the afternoon, or

… L1 is used in the classroom and English in the gym.

Children, at this stage, learn another language much as they have learnt, and are learning, L1. This principle is fundamental when deciding how to teach them a foreign language.

1 Write a list of at least five learning characteristics that are specific to children.

2 How do these characteristics influence the activities you would choose for your pupils? List some activities you have used or plan to use that are adapted to these learning characteristics.

3 Now look at the list in the next section and compare it with your own. Are there any characteristics you would like to add to this list?

Children's main learning characteristics – and their implications

- Children are energetic. They need to move a lot.
- Children are noisy. You can't expect a quiet class with young children, especially if you are trying to teach a spoken language! It's more a matter of controlling the noise level (getting them not to speak too loudly) and teaching them, little by little, to have 'quiet' times as well. Allow them be noisy in a positive way by getting them to play action games, and by letting them speak to each other in class while they are working.
- Children are quick – quick to learn and quick to forget! You will need to constantly revise what you have taught.
- Children like to use their senses as well as to speak. They need to see, hear, touch, smell and taste.
- Children have imagination. Use it.
- Children are fun and enthusiastic. Have fun and be enthusiastic with them and everyone will benefit!
- Children are children. Don't expect too much. Everything comes with time.

CHAPTER 1

Children's development

The chart below outlines children's basic development, from three to six years old, and from six to nine years old. It aims to show what you can and cannot expect from children in these age groups, and how you can teach them in ways that are appropriate for their stage of development. Remember that these are just general guidelines, and that there can be great differences between individual children.

Child development			
Areas of development	**Ages**		**Educational implications**
	3–6	**6–9**	
Control of muscular movement	• Still developing, so a great need for physical exercise.	• Muscles are stronger and more resistant. • Control of body is greater.	• Activities should be varied and should help develop large motor movements (running, jumping, etc.) and hand–eye coordination (cutting out, modelling, etc.). • Teacher should remember that physical changes can generate insecurity.
Emotions	• Very unstable: can have sudden tantrums and whims. • Feels both insecurity and omnipotence. • Does not know how to wait, which causes frustration.	• Begins to cooperate with others. • Has greater control of emotional ambivalence. • Is interested in sexual differences.	• Activities should be short, with lots of variety. • Teacher should be warm, well balanced and able to restore child's equilibrium. Should offer constant encouragement.
Intelligence	• Symbolic thought begins (can substitute drawing or game for real object). • Thought is subjective and egocentric. • Confuses fantasy and reality.	• Is more realistic and rational. • Becomes more objective. • Discovers coincidence. • Opens up to the outside world.	• Activities should use toys that imitate real life (toy cars, toy food, etc.). • Activities for 6–9 year-olds should widen their minds and develop reasoning and logic, as well as creativity and imagination.
Language	• Can express himself clearly in L1 by age 3–4.	• Uses tenses correctly at age 6; understands them from age 8–9.	• Activities should develop oral and writing skills.

Areas of development	Ages		Educational implications
	3–6	**6–9**	
Sociability	• Is egocentric, subjective and dependent. • First contacts with peers are ambivalent (can be aggressive and friendly to same person). • Starts to be aware of his potential (both abilities and limitations). • Plays parallel to others.	• Initiates relationships with peers. • Alternates periods of silence and continuous talking. • Can work very simply in a team from age 7–8. • Needs the group for security and self-esteem. • Learns moral values from adults.	• Teacher should favour group work to encourage sociability, sharing and concentration. • With 6–9 year-olds, teacher should be concerned with their scale of values. • Teacher should know that conflict with adults is normal with older age group.
Behaviour	• Extremely keen to communicate, in order to differentiate himself from others. • Passionate and non-systematic in ways he does things. • Does not always want to do suggested activity. • Physically aggressive, without a motive. • Takes other children's toys as a way of affirming himself. • Interrupts activities to gain attention.	• Very active child starts to become calmer. • Usually keen to read and write. • Often admires teachers and thinks they know everything.	• Teacher should encourage communication. • Teacher should persuade child to do required activity (e.g. suggest he does it later). • Teacher should monitor aggressive behaviour, without over-reacting. • Teacher should try to be good role model for older children.

CHAPTER 2

Getting organised

Classroom resources

You will probably find it useful to gradually build up a set of materials to use in your classroom for:

... creative activities, e.g. crayons for drawing

... storing items like books or pens, e.g. boxes

... helping the children identify items that belong to them, e.g. labelling them.

1 If you are new to teaching young children, what kinds of items do you think will be useful for working with them? List ten items. (Think of the categories above.)

Or, if you are experienced with this age group, what are the ten items you have found most useful when working with them?

Do not look at the lists below.

2 When you have written your list, read the lists of resources below and tick those items which you mentioned in your own list.

Resources for activities

- Crayons, pencils, felt-tip pens (with non-permanent ink), round-tipped scissors.
- Paints (see that they are washable!) and thick and fine paintbrushes.
- Glue sticks. They are much cleaner to use than paste or glue in a bottle.
- Wide and narrow sellotape; double-sided sellotape.
- Coloured card for backing pictures, making FLASHCARDS, crafts, etc.
- Large pieces of paper for making murals, displaying class projects, etc.
- Magazines and comics which children can cut out to make pictures, FLASHCARDS, collages, etc.
- Rolls of transparent adhesive plastic covering to protect homemade cards and FLASHCARDS.
- Old newspapers to cover tables or floor when doing messy activities. (Ask your pupils to bring them in.)
- A washing line and clothes pegs are useful for some games, for hanging up artwork to dry or exhibit, or for plays.
- An old sheet can be hung on the washing line as the stage curtains, or used as something to pin scenery on to make a backdrop, or for more games.
- If you can spare the room, it can be worth asking the children at the beginning of the school year to bring in things like empty toilet rolls, wool, buttons, bits of material, pipe cleaners, etc. to have on hand for crafts.

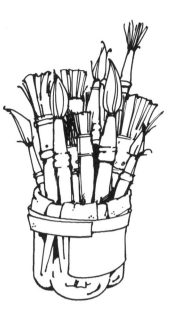

Resources for storage

- Large plastic bottles, with the tops cut off, make handy containers for scissors, pencils, paintbrushes, etc. Cover the cut-off edges with masking tape so children do not cut themselves.
- Envelopes to keep your own and the children's FLASHCARDS in.
- Shoe boxes for storing envelopes, or other objects. Draw a picture on the front of what is kept in the shoe box.
- A few big boxes to hold toys, Lego, etc. (depending on the age of your children). Cover them in coloured wrapping paper and put a picture on the front or top of what is kept inside.

Resources for identification

- With younger children, you can tie different coloured ribbons onto scissors, or other objects. Children identify their group's scissors by the ribbons (scissors with green ribbons are for the green group).
- With older children, you can write their names on a piece of ribbon and then tie it on the various objects.

Classroom language

At the start of the school year, choose a few expressions of simple classroom language to teach your pupils. If you repeat the expressions every time you do a particular activity, the children will soon understand them. As the year progresses, you can gradually introduce new ones.

In the lists on PHOTOCOPIABLE PAGES 1–2 you will find useful language for:

… general class management

… common classroom materials

… action games

… board games

… card games

… songs.

1. Read through the lists on PHOTOCOPIABLE PAGES 1–2 and translate any expressions that are new to you. Write the translation next to the English expression. Where possible, use simple drawings to help you remember the meaning.
2. From time to time, return to the lists and test yourself on the new expressions.

    Add any other expressions that you often use in L1. Find the English equivalent and try to use that in class instead.
3. Show the list to another teacher. Ask them to add expressions that they use.
4. Choose ten expressions from the lists to teach your class (not all at once). When will you use them?

CHAPTER 3

Managing your class

This chapter looks at how to:

… manage your class of very young children

… how to give them an environment in which they can learn and feel safe

… establish an atmosphere of order and intimacy.

"What is the importance of classroom layout?"

The layout of a classroom can influence the classroom atmosphere, by creating, for example, feelings of togetherness or isolation. It can also affect the effectiveness of your teaching. For example, when you are teaching a language, it is essential that everyone can see your lips when you are speaking so they can see how you shape new sounds.

A useful and versatile way to arrange the class is to place the tables and chairs in a 'U' shape. This means that:

… the children can see you perfectly

… the children have a sense of togetherness

… you can create a more intimate area for storytelling or singing, if you sit your pupils on the floor in a circle within the 'U'

… you can put the children into pairs or groups by simply taking some chairs from the outside of the 'U' and placing them on the inside

… you can go from child to child, sitting opposite each one, moving freely within the 'U'. (Remember to look after your back and take a chair with you!)

… the outside of the 'U' provides natural corners for a library area, PROJECT CENTRE, or place to play cards, etc.

… there is space for the children to play, skip and run around the 'U'.

Using these different spaces within the class gives a sense of change and of doing something different and new. You can also create a sense of closeness by moving the children away from their desks. For example, singing a song sitting at your desk is not the same as sitting on the floor together in an intimate circle.

While this 'U' shape layout is very useful, it is a good idea to have a break from routine from time to time by changing the layout.

Group work

Whatever the layout of your classroom, it can be useful to divide your class into smaller, more manageable sub-groups. This can be especially helpful with pupils aged three to five.

Working in groups gives children the opportunity to learn to:

… work as a team and help each other

… identify and look after their material. This is easier for them if they can share the responsibility among the group. SEE ROTATING TASKS PAGE 13

Colour-coding

You can give each group a colour so that you can:

… easily mobilise different groups. e.g. *Blue group, go to the library corner. Red and yellow groups, come here, please.*

… rotate activities and tasks. Make charts with symbols of activities or tasks, colour-coded according to group. For example, draw a picture of a crayon with a red circle next to it. From this, the children in the red group know they are going to do colouring.

… assign responsibility for colour-coded items to the different colour groups.

Rotating tasks

● A good way to organise the tidying up at the end of a lesson ◆ SEE TIDYING UP PAGE 14 is to make different colour groups responsible for certain tasks during a certain week. For example, one week the blue group has to see that the toys are all put away before going home, the red group has to see that the library corner is neat, etc. You can make a wallchart with pictures representing different tasks, with coloured circles showing which groups are responsible for the tasks.

● Put colour codes on the pencil pots and scissors so that each group can identify their items. ◆ SEE RESOURCES FOR STORAGE/IDENTIFICATION PAGE 11 They can then learn to take responsibility for them and to share that responsibility with the other members of their group. They can also learn from each other how to tidy up.

● When a table is left in a mess, it's much easier to say *Blue group, your table, please!* than to try and find the individual(s) who didn't clean up. You will avoid the typical 'I didn't do it' situation and often the children will sort the problem out by themselves within their group.

Children can manage themselves

With children aged five and older, you can get them to manage themselves when they are doing an activity in groups. Do this by assigning roles before the activity. For example, before playing a game of memory ◆ SEE PAGE 49, you can make one or two pupils 'English teachers', who have to remind everyone to speak in English and who should help to correct the others in the group. There can be a 'judge' who has to see that no one cheats, a 'head of cleaning' who is responsible for materials and checks that the rest of the group has put the cards away at the end of the game, etc.

Do not always choose the most proficient pupils to be the 'English teachers'. When you select slower students for this role, spend a few minutes apart with them if you can, to explain their task. They will make a special effort to perform well.

Monitoring groups

Go round the classroom to check that each group is working. When groups are playing a quiet game, check occasionally that everyone in each group is participating and paying attention. Get the whole group to chant a question or say *It's your turn!*

Class routine

It is important with young children to have a class routine. Young children have no sense of formal time, so saying *20 minutes* means nothing to them, but a routine helps them to know what to expect and do and starts giving them a notion of time passing.

Beginning the lesson

Always begin the lesson with the same routine. Use an activity which will both draw the class together and make them realise that the English lesson has begun, such as a song or rhyme that they know well. ◆ SEE CHAPTER 7 PAGES 54–61 Never start with anything new.

Then, for example, revise a few items of vocabulary (with pictures) and add one or two new ones. Or ask them a question that they know but have not heard with those pictures. This will prepare them for learning something new.

Bringing work to an end

If the children are working on something and the lesson is soon going to end, warn them. It is very frustrating for a child to have to stop without warning in the middle of an interesting activity. You can say, for example *Please finish your work now. We are going to clean up in five minutes*. A few minutes later say *All right children, put away your things, it's time to clean up*.

Tidying up

- It is very important that children learn to look after their things and tidy up after themselves.

- Always allot some time at the end of your lesson for cleaning up. If you do not do this consistently, you may find yourself cleaning up after the lesson and that the children are not learning to become responsible.

- Have specific corners, shelves and boxes for different things: you can wrap a cardboard box in wrapping paper, glue a picture of a doll on the side of the 'doll' box, or tape a pencil to the front of the drawer of the 'pencil drawer', etc. ◆ SEE PAGE 11

- When the whole class is untidy, it is effective and fun to say *I am going to count to 10, and when I get to 10, I want the classroom to be tidy. Ready?* Raise your hand and put up your fingers as you count. *One, two, three …* See that everyone participates!

- Never let your pupils leave without having put away their personal possessions and tidied up the classroom.

Finishing the lesson

Always finish the lesson with the same routine so that the children realise that the lesson has finished. For example, you can say *Put your chairs on the table and make a line at the door, please*. Once at the door, ask each child or pair of children a question before leaving. Or you can ask all the children to sit down and say *People with brown shoes can go*. The children with brown shoes place their chairs neatly on or under the tables and leave. (Or, for example *People who can play football can go*, etc.)

Materials

- See that everyone has everything they need before starting an activity and always have extra materials ready for the child who needs to start again or who has left his materials at home.

- Always have more materials available than necessary. You will need them for when a class works very quickly or for those children who always finish before the others. A child with nothing to do is a potential source of trouble, so have extra pictures to colour, puzzles to do, cards to play with or books to look at.

Leaving the classroom

The idea of leaving the classroom is always exciting for young children. Explain to your pupils what you are going to do and where you are going. Get them to stand in a line and explain that other classes are working so they must be quiet and not run. If they do, tell them to go straight back and start again. An action is worth a thousand words.

Tell very young pupils that they are something quiet (butterflies, fairies, etc.) to get them to walk silently down the corridor. This also teaches them some new vocabulary!

Going to the toilet

You will find that when one child asks to go to the toilet or to get a drink, everyone else suddenly wants to go, too.

- With the very young, it is easier to get them all in a line in front of the toilet with you at the head of the line, sitting on a small chair (remember your back!), as you will have to help them undress and then get dressed again. Afterwards, you will be able to work in peace for a while. Your children will have to learn, little by little, to wait for the toilet and not to interrupt the class every few minutes. Of course, when they do ask to go, you should profit from the situation and insist they ask in English.

- With five- to seven-year-olds, allow only one child out at a time, although you may need to let shy children be accompanied by a friend at first.

Be sensitive to the mood of the class

There will be days when the class is so tired or excited that they are impossible to work with, so don't! Be flexible. Have other activities ready for these occasions. If the children are tired, let them colour a picture, for example, while you go from child to child. If they are excited, take them outside and play an energetic action game. ◈ SEE CHAPTER 5

Giving rewards

When a child has worked well or made a special effort, it is important to reward him to show that you value his achievement. A reward does not have to be elaborate. You can draw a smiley face next to his exercise, shake his hand or hit the palm of your hand against his (a 'high five'), with the verbal congratulation *Well done!* or *Good for you!* The physical element makes the *Good for you!* into something special and makes your pupil feel close to you.

Remember to congratulate a child on his personal progress. He may learn more slowly or more quickly than others in the class. It is important to reward both the slow and the fast learner for real effort and hard work.

Discipline

"Why is my whole class difficult?"

A class that loves its teacher will, on the whole, work for that teacher. However, external events affect young children more than older ones. Take into account that:

… your class will be excited and difficult to deal with when the weather is about to change

… at the end of the day, week or term, children will be tired and excited, so lighten the work load

... anything new or different will enthuse children and make them difficult to handle (but their pleasure and pride at the end of a new activity make it worth the effort)

... children may be troublesome either because they have not really understood what you are expecting them to do, or they are bored, or the activity is too long. In that case, it is easier to stop the activity and return to it another day when you have had a chance to re-plan it.

"What can I do when my class is difficult?"

- Shouting at a class to get its attention is a short term, very limited approach and one which sets a bad example (although an occasional shout will not hurt when necessary). Other methods to try are as follows:

- Use a well-established signal which means *Children, be quiet and pay attention*. For example, clap three times and put up your hand, saying nothing. As the children see you, they should put up their hands and be quiet. Little by little, silence will spread.
  For younger children, you could ring a little bell which means they have to show you their work. Then say *You are speaking too loudly. Do you know how to whisper? Let's practise: How are you?... Good. Now continue like that.*

- If the class is restless, use a favourite game as an incentive: *If you finish quickly, we'll play ...*

- Some days are impossible. Forget your lesson plan and go outside and let the children play. You can make use of these days by calling the children over to you one by one, or in pairs, for individual speaking time and attention. This is a good opportunity to assess and record their progress, which will help when it is time to write reports. ◆ SEE RECORDING PUPILS' PROGRESS PAGE 18 It is also an excellent activity when you yourself are not performing as well as normal and you want to give yourself a break.

- A last resort is to 'hypnotise' the class. If you have already played the game to teach adjectives ◆ SEE PAGE 72, you are ready to do this. Just say *One, two, three, sleep!* and the children will react by habit and pretend they are sleeping by putting their heads on their desks and being quiet. (No giggling or snoring allowed – this is serious.) When they have calmed down, speak to them calmly and quietly, then let them 'sleep' a little more before continuing. If they rush into the next activity, they have to go back to sleep again. Don't worry if they spend a good part of your lesson 'sleeping': what you lose in time you will gain in training them in concentration and discipline. Children always prefer to do something instead of sleeping, and, given a choice (*Do you want to sleep or ... ?*), they will choose the latter.

- If the class is restless, it is sometimes effective to ask *Who are the best children in the school?* and when they have calmed down: *I know you are the best. Very good.*

- Remember to praise the children when they have been good: *You are working hard and are learning a lot. I'm very proud of you.*

"How do I discipline individual children?"

Individual discipline is exactly that: individual. With time, you will learn what works best with each child.

- If a child is disruptive just walk over to him and place your hand on his shoulder or head and continue with the lesson.

- Likewise, if two or three children are misbehaving, just place yourself physically in their midst.

- If you are sitting on the floor while doing an activity with young children, place the disruptive child on your lap or right beside you, and continue with the activity. There is no need to tell them to stop talking. Your proximity is enough to silence them and you have not interrupted the activity.

"How do I speak to a young child about his misbehaviour?"

When you have to speak personally to a child about an incident of misbehaviour, it is better to tell him you want to speak to him after class. When you are on your own with him, get down to his level (squat, in other words) and speak to him face to face, holding his hand or putting your hand on his shoulder or hip. That way:

… you will communicate with him more easily

… the child will be obliged to pay attention

… you are showing your concern and the importance of what you are saying.

If a normally cooperative child suddenly starts misbehaving, there is usually a reason fo this: for example, his parents have separated, his mother is expecting or has just had a baby, the family is moving, etc. Find out what is happening and take it into account.

Remember that a child that constantly misbehaves is very often a discouraged child that needs help and attention.

Preventive discipline

The most effective way to teach a child to behave is through 'preventive discipline'. This, however, takes time and practice. For example:

- Maria is writing on her desk. You can say *Maria, I see that you feel like writing. Let me give you some paper to write on and that way the desk won't get dirty*.
- Damian is drumming with his pencil on the desk. He is making a noise and bothering his fellow pupils. You can say *Damian, you are good at drumming! You've got good rhythm. Let's see if after class you can show the class and me what you can do. We'd like to hear you but not now because everyone is working.*

In other words, instead of reprimanding a child, you are telling him that there is a time, a place and a way for everything and you are showing him how to do this particular action in an acceptable way.

"What can I do with quiet children?"

Some children are very shy and quiet and need to grow in confidence. It is easier to try and help them feel more self-confident through physical activities before trying to get them to speak in English.

- Tell a colleague that you are going to send a specific child to her on an errand. Send the child with a friend to your colleague's class with some chalk. Your colleague will thank him kindly. Later ask the child *Do you think you can take this message to Mrs …? I think you can.* If he says *No*, respect his answer and send him with someone else, but prepare him little by little. One day, with your encouragement, he will give it a try. Your message might end up in a wastepaper basket or, at best, left in front of your colleague's door without a knock on the door, but he has taken some important first steps towards greater self-confidence.
- If your shy child needs to go to the toilet, send him with a friend. When that seems all right, send him on his own.

- In class, carefully place your shy child with children who are open but who won't overwhelm him.
- Give him opportunities to do things in front of others. e.g. *Do you want to sing a song with me for the class? No? Well, how about you and me singing a song with Teresa?*
- Use physical opportunities so that the child can start enjoying being the centre of attention. Make sure that at the beginning his role is not demanding.
- When it comes to speaking in class, even seven- and eight-year-olds can 'lose' their voices occasionally, especially if they have to speak in another language. They will whisper their answer and you will have to sit right beside them and strain to hear them. When they have given a good answer say *Very good! Now how about telling your friend beside you?* and later *How about telling the answer to the class? Your friends would like to know.*
- Do not let yourself get absorbed by your noisier, more outgoing pupils: your shy pupils need time, and lots of encouragement and opportunities to grow in self-confidence.

"What can I do with active children?"

Here, we are referring to children who need a lot of activity, not naughty children. These children learn to slow down and acquire longer concentration spans as they get older, but in the meantime:

… always have extra activities to give them, especially ones that will help them learn to concentrate

… disguise the fact that you are just keeping them busy: *Anna, do you think you could do this puzzle for me? I need to know if there are any pieces missing.* Or *Do you think you could colour this poster for the class?* etc.

… make them feel that they are doing something useful and that they are helping, not annoying, you.

Recording pupils' progress

Whether a requirement or not, it is very useful to keep a record of your pupils' progress.

"When should I assess my pupils' progress?"

- It is a good idea, two or three times during the school year, to sit the pupils beside you, either individually or in pairs, to assess their progress.
- You will need about five or ten minutes per child to do this exercise, depending on the child.
- Use a day when the class is particularly excited and is unable to work, or when you yourself are having a bad day. (We all have them!) Let the class play either in the classroom or the playground while you call each child to you. You are giving your children a break from routine as well as getting some valuable information on your class and individual pupils.
- Or take time while the children are busy doing something quiet to call them over individually.
- Or spend a few minutes after the lesson with an individual pupil.
- If you find a child is having a bad day, let him do the exercise another time.

"How should I assess my pupils' progress?"

For example, show the child a picture on the subject you want to check and ask him to describe it. In the child's notebook, write the date and what he is saying.

Be sure to record faithfully what he says. Note:

… if he corrects himself

… if he does not complete a word (for example, *mo-*)

… if you have to help him with a word

… if his fluency or pronunciation has improved

… anything else of relevance (e.g. is he starting to create his own sentences?).

Do not worry about noting down every grammatical or lexical error.

Try not to help your pupils unless it is really essential. Some children get 'stuck' if they cannot find the word they want; others simply cannot think of anything to say. Help them by asking questions, miming an action, etc. and encourage them throughout the exercise.

Here is an example of such an assessment. It is of Isabel, who is six years old. It was made at the beginning of her second year of English. The class had been learning about animals and the teacher asked Isabel to talk about the picture of the jungle that she was colouring. (The rest of the class was busy colouring the same picture too.)

First the teacher put Isabel at ease by commenting that her picture was very pretty: *What's this, Isabel? It's a jungle. That's right. Good! Now, what can you see in the jungle?*

Isabel: *The jungle is big. In the jungle is monkeys, elephants and lions. In the wat—* (The teacher wrote what Isabel said and added *water* in brackets.) *is a hippo. The hippo is fat and red.* (Isabel had coloured her hippo red.) *He, hippo, swimming. One parrot flying. The gorilla is pretty. He is behind the elephant. In front the elephant is lion, giraffe and kangaroo. A giraffe is hungry. A tiger is orange. I love the picture.*

The teacher wrote:

Improvements: *is/are*, prepositions

Problems: *a/the there is/are*

Fluency: Improved a lot.

Early the following term the teacher assessed Isabel's progress again. This time she used a story about nature. ◈ SEE PAGE 44 The class had worked on the story a couple of weeks before. The teacher asked the class to try and remember the story and draw it. While they did so, she went around the classroom assessing some of the pupils.

Teacher: *Isabel, tell me the story of the witch.*

Isabel: *There is a witch. She is hungry. She has got one …* (L1 for *broom*). (Teacher underlined the word written in L1.) *She is on the mountains. She going to fly in the sky. She going to visit in the moon.* (Teacher underlined *moon* since Isabel didn't remember the word.) *She is hungry. She is going to eating a boys. Boys live in the house in the fields. There are one bear in the cave. In the cave, there is fire. There is a path. On the path is a …*(witch). *A bear is catching the … *(witch). *There is a bear throwing the witch in the river.*

The teacher wrote her comments in Isabel's notebook. Isabel was curious and asked *What does it say?*

Teacher: *It says you speak very good English.*

Isabel was pleased, naturally.

To a weaker student you could say *It says you are making a lot of progess and I am very happy*, or *It says your work isn't too bad but I think you can work harder*. Since the children see it written down (they can't read it because they are too young) they give your comment a lot of importance.

It is interesting to get your pupils to do this exercise with the same picture twice, at different times of the year.

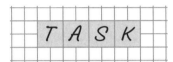

From the extract above, how would you assess Isabel's use of *a/the*, *-ing* verbs and verbs with *going to*? Write a brief assessment, and then check with the teacher's comments. ◆ SEE KEY PAGE 90.

"Why should I keep a record of my pupils' work?"

These records will be useful in many ways.

- You will be able to see exactly where each pupil is having problems.
- You will get a general view of what the class has and hasn't assimilated and what needs working on.
- Children love to see what they have said on paper. It encourages them: *Did I say all that in English? Wow!*
- You have something to show parents when they come to see you and you will be able to explain to them perfectly how their child is doing. (Parents will feel proud to see that their children are able to say something in English.)
- You have a record which you can use when you have to write reports.
- And finally, you yourself will feel encouraged when you read your pupils' notebooks. There are periods during the school year when you can feel that your pupils are just not progressing, which is a very frustrating, if not depressing, feeling. However, if you go back to the beginning of your pupils' notebooks and look through them, you will see that you are wrong and that your children are in fact improving.

To remind yourself of all the tips in this chapter, cover the text and read only the questions in the margin. Can you remember the advice?

CHAPTER 4

Teaching young children a language

This chapter outlines a few basic principles to consider when you are teaching a foreign language to young children.

Speaking

- Speak at normal speed (unless you speak very quickly). It will take the children a little longer to start hearing separate words, but soon they will be able to understand English spoken at a normal rate.
- Do not break up your sentences thinking you are helping your pupils identify individual words: use normal stress and intonation. Remember that children at this stage learn by imitation.
- Use English whenever possible. All your instructions and questions (e.g. *Make two groups. Don't cheat. Wipe your nose. Where's Raul? Is he ill?*) are just as important as what you want to teach.
- Use full sentences or phrases. When your pupils are describing pictures, insist that they use full sentences. For example, in answer to the question *What's this?* they should say *It's a ball*, not just *ball*. If you are teaching colours, teach *a yellow banana* and *a red apple*. Some children may answer *Yellow banana* to the question *What colour is the ball?* but they will quickly correct themselves as they learn unconsciously to place the article and adjective in front of the noun. By using full sentences or phrases, children:

  … get a sense of context

  … assimilate the different syntaxes and structures which they will be able to use later when they begin creating their own sentences.

  … find it just as easy to use a sentence or phrase as a word.

Children learn at different rates

Strangely enough, it is accepted that children are allowed a period of silence before they start using L1 yet they are usually expected to start speaking straight away when they are learning a foreign language. You will find that, in fact, some children will begin using their English right away (especially if they already speak a second language) while others will need at least a term, if not a whole school year to start using the language. The difference in maturity among very young children of the same class can be enormous. Be patient. They will speak! Usually girls, musical children and children who already speak more than one language, learn a new language more quickly and more easily than the others.

Listening

When you teach a new structure or vocabulary item, let your pupils listen to you and watch you as you speak and mime, or speak and point. Do this several times if necessary. Then get the children to copy your gestures while you repeat the structure or word. Finally, get them to join in with you. Have a gesture to indicate to your pupils when they should repeat after you, so that you can control the rhythm of the exercise. For example, you could simply point at them in a deliberate way. Remember that it is always helpful if your pupils have already heard you use the language you are teaching. In other words, when you are speaking in class, do not be afraid of using new structures, tenses or vocabulary before you actually teach them.

Finally, it is extremely important to remember that children need a long time before the language they understand becomes language they can use (before 'passive' language becomes 'active'). It is easy to say *Do you understand? Good.* and then go on to something new, forgetting that your pupils need to practise the language a lot more and to hear it used in different contexts before they can assimilate it enough to use it.

Using L1 – 'sandwiching'

When, how often and how much should you use L1 with young children?

Compare your answers with other teachers in your school, if possible. Then compare your answers and theirs with the advice given below.

- If you use L1 to give a short instruction or to translate a word, 'sandwich' it: in other words, use the English, then L1, then repeat in English. (*Sleep!* L1 for *sleep, Sleep!*)

- You are going to need L1, especially at the beginning when setting discipline and class rules or at any time when you would waste too much time explaining an activity in English. But do use the expressions you are going to need to manage the class right from the start. ◈ SEE PHOTOCOPIABLE PAGES 1–2. Children will quickly begin to understand them and to use them themselves and you create an English 'atmosphere' right from the beginning.

- Use L1 less and less as the school year progresses.

- Once you see that a child can use certain expressions more or less correctly, be firm and consistent in getting him to use them. Do not let him use L1 instead. Some children will constantly test you over this. If they do not remember to use English, then:

  … ask them to ask a friend how to say the word, phrase or sentence and then come back to you with it

  … encourage them to think about it. (e.g. *You know how to say it, come on!*) If it is urgent (e.g. going to the toilet) you can prompt them, but do not let them get into the habit of waiting for your prompt.

- Children never realise how much they know. Very often, they think they know very little since their parents mistakenly expect them to know very little, because they are so young.

- Try to be aware of how often you use L1 in the classroom. It is so easy to fall into the habit of doing so and children quickly learn to just wait for your instructions in it, unwilling to make the effort to understand you in English.

- If you feel you are using L1 too much, it may be useful, as a reminder to yourself, to put up a sign at the back of the class that says *Speak in English*.

Try to notice what you often say in L1 in your lessons. Can you teach the English equivalent of these phrases or sentences so that you do not have to use L1 so much? Did you actually realise you were using L1? Why did you use it? Could you have made yourself understood in English with a little more effort?

• Do not worry if your English is not perfect or especially good. Most primary teachers in the world are not fluent English speakers but they still do a very good job of teaching young children the language. At this level, children need more than anything to learn to like the language, and this should be your main objective. This does not mean that they will not learn very much – they will, and you will be surprised by how much they learn – but they have years ahead of them to perfect the language. If you give them the early experience of learning English in an affectionate atmosphere and through activities they enjoy, there is a good chance that your pupils will do well in English later.

Pronunciation

Young children need to 'hear' the different sounds in a foreign language, hence the importance of working with rhymes and songs and of listening to taped material as much as possible, right from the beginning. Good pronunciation comes gradually as the children learn to distinguish different sounds.

• Do not over-correct pronunciation. Instead, focus on a particular sound and ask the children to pronounce it one by one. This should help them to really hear it.

• Pay special attention to the English sounds that are problematic for speakers of a particular language. For example, distinguishing the /ɪ/ and /iː/ for native speakers of Latin languages, the /æ/ for native German speakers, etc. Even if you cannot pronounce the sounds yourself, be aware of these difficulties and use tapes to provide models of pronunciation.

• Make sure that your pupils see your lips when you speak. Different facial muscles are used for speaking different languages.

• The ability to pronounce specific sounds in L1 can come as late as four or five years old. (If a child is already bilingual, there may be interference and he may need a little longer to perfect his ability.) It is perfectly normal for a young child not to be able to pronounce certain sounds in L1 and the same will occur in English. The majority of children will get over this problem as they get older. If you think there is a serious problem, speak to the class teacher (if you are only in charge of English) or the speech specialist.

Actions and mime

Young children use their bodies spontaneously and identify physically with the world around them. Make the most of this by using lots of mime and action. Mime and action help to:

… communicate what you are saying

… keep the children's attention

… reinforce words and structures

… correct your pupils and/or to prompt them. You will find that your pupils will use these actions while speaking until they are so sure of what they are saying that they unconsciously drop the action.

The use or non-use of actions is a way of measuring how much a pupil has assimilated a word or structure.

Keeping your pupils' attention

• Children have very short attention spans. Make your activities short and change them often.

• Children are energetic and need to move. Change the pace of your activities by following games with lots of physical movement, with quieter, less active ones.

Hello! How are you?

Fine, thank you.

- During the term, teach the same thing over again in as many different ways possible (although you can use the same game several times as children love to play the same game over and over again).
- Maintain good eye contact with the whole class.
- Vary the way you speak (speak loudly, whisper, use a high or low voice, etc.).
- Use lots of action and mime. Exaggerate facial expressions.
- Get your pupils to participate actively by interrupting yourself and asking questions. e.g. '... and the wolf ate the cake ...' Show me how he ate the cake. Ready? (Children pretend to eat a cake.) And what do you think he is going to do?
- Children are tactile so let them touch, feel, throw and make things. Take REALIA and pictures into your class for them to touch.
- Use puppets, not only to keep your children's attention but also to get them to speak. Often little ones do not dare speak to you, but they will to a puppet. Or, they are too shy to speak but, if they have a puppet on their hand, they will make the puppet speak.
- Relax and enjoy your class. If pupils feel that you are enjoying yourself, they will participate more actively and pay more attention.

Correcting

Correcting children is a fundamental skill which comes with time and practice. A child who is corrected inappropriately can lose confidence, fluency and the ability to correct himself. He may simply wait for your corrections every time he speaks. Remember that at this stage, we are trying to get pupils to like the language and to use it as intuitively and as fluently as possible as a means of communication. Here are some guidelines.

- Avoid correcting your pupils in the middle of a sentence. You will hamper their fluency.
- Sometimes, however, if you feel your pupil knows better, you might interrupt him and repeat the sentence up to the mistake. Then let your pupil continue while correcting himself. For example, Eric says Anna have got and you interrupt saying Anna ... . Eric should correct himself and finish the sentence: Anna has got a cat. This is good practice for stronger pupils and weaker students can see that even the best pupils make mistakes.
- Do not correct constantly. Pupils will be afraid to speak.
- Only correct the most important mistake(s), depending on what you are teaching and if communication breaks down as a result of the mistake.
- Correct in a positive way. Correct by repeating, for example. A pupil says Anna have got a cat. Teacher: Oh, Anna has got a cat, has she? That's nice. You are correcting him imperceptibly and showing interest in what he is saying.
- Use actions. If you have been using a specific action to illustrate and reinforce a word or structure, use it to correct. If you point vigorously in front of you every time you use go and a child asks Can I have a toilet, please?, say: Can I ... ? and point vigorously in front of you. Your pupil will automatically correct himself.

- Use their sense of humour to let them see what a funny thing they have said. If a pupil says *Can I have a toilet, please?*, answer *Yes. You can have a toilet. Here!* Pretend you are giving your pupil Something Very Big! Your pupil will usually understand that what he said was not what he meant and correct himself with a laugh. Or, if a pupil shows you a drawing of a monster and says *Your name is Fernando*, look very surprised and answer *No! My name is … !*

- An interesting way to correct, to be used once in a while when your pupils have finished speaking, is to let them compare two structures and ask them to tell you which 'sounds right' to them. If one pupil has said *He has got hair brown*, ask him *What sounds better: 'He has got hair brown', or 'He has got brown hair'?* Invariably, the child will know (will 'feel') which is correct as, deep-down, he has assimilated the structure. Children who have been learning English over a certain period should learn to listen to their intuition instead of their intellect. This goes especially for older children who invariably start translating when they begin to read and write.

- And last, but certainly not least: If your pupils love you – and young children will give you their hearts – they will learn, no matter what.

A checklist of correcting techniques

- Only correct the mistake(s) that are important.
- Give the correct form as a natural part of your next sentence but without drawing your pupil's attention to his mistake.
- Repeat the sentence up to the part where your pupil has made the mistake and let him correct himself (to be used only if you are sure that your pupil knows what is wrong).
- Use actions to prompt correct answers.
- Ask pupils to listen to two versions and let them decide which is correct.
- Take what your pupil has said literally, so that he realises that something is wrong.

In your next lesson, try and notice how you correct your pupils. Think about these questions:

1. Do you tend to tell your pupils that what they said is 'not right'? Are you correcting your pupils positively?

2. Why do you correct the way you do? For the pupil who has made the mistake, or for the rest of the class?

3. Did the pupils notice the corrections?

4. Did they learn anything from them?

5. Do you use the most appropriate methods of correction for your pupils?
   a. In the short term?
   b. In the longer term?

CHAPTER 5

Action games

Playing is a child's natural way of learning. A game with all its rules and interaction is a mini social world in which children prepare themselves, little by little, to enter society. Through games and play, children learn to accept rules (e.g. not to cheat), how to work with others and how to behave (e.g. how to lose) – all in an enjoyable atmosphere. Games also develop the child's automatic use of a foreign language, coordination, cognitive thought, etc.

Think about the use of games when teaching a foreign language. What are the advantages of using them compared with a traditional teaching method? Compare your ideas with those in the list below.

Why use games?

In teaching a language to children, games are ideal for the following reasons.

- Language and activity is an authentic combination for these learners – it is one they use in L1.
- The language used in games is repetitive and/or uses basic structures.
- There is a real purpose for using the language.
- Children tend to forget they are learning and so use the language spontaneously.
- As children will happily play games again and again, they are ideal for practising new vocabulary and structures and for varying with different language.
- Games create a sense of closeness within the class.

"What are the criteria for choosing games?"

Here are some things to consider when choosing a game for your class.

- The game should be relevant linguistically.
- It should be simple to explain, set up and play.
- Everyone should be able to participate in it.
- It should be fun.

Tips for playing games

"How do I set up a game?"

Teaching children a new game, even a simple one, can be difficult. Try to use English phrases and vocabulary such as *Make two groups, You're out*, etc.
◆ SEE PHOTOCOPIABLE PAGE 2. But you will often have to use a combination of L1 and English, using English for the easier and/or the most important expressions.
◆ SEE PAGE 22 When your pupils understand what they have to do in the game, use English.

Here are some ways of showing children what to do in a game. Choose the most suitable one for the game you want to play.

- Play the game with one or two pupils in front of the class as a demonstration.
- With card games, tell the children to sit around you in a circle on the floor, so they can see the cards better while you explain.
- If the game is to be played in a large area, place the children where they should be to play. Then act out both the part of 'it' (the person who has to chase the others or lead the action) and the part of the pupils so that the children can see what they are supposed to do.
- Always have several trials before starting a new game and tell the children they are trials. Some children get very upset when fellow pupils do not seem to play the game properly, but if you tell them it is just a trial, they will be more patient.
- When you really do play the game, you may like to give each child one opportunity before they are 'out' so that competitive children do not get upset and so the game lasts longer.
- Give the game a chance. Sometimes a new game does not seem to work, but do not be discouraged. Try it again another time and as they understand it better, you will find that the children begin to enjoy it, and it may even become a favourite.
- Some children, even at a very young age, are highly competitive, so it is a good idea to let two or three children be the winners instead of just one. Likewise, in many games, several children can be eliminated at the same time.
- Young children often fall, hurt themselves and come crying to you (usually there is nothing wrong with them, fortunately). Don't ignore them. It is quicker to say *Oh, dear. That hurts, doesn't it?*, give them a little sympathetic pat on the shoulder and send them off to play. You have given them the bit of attention that they wanted so they are happy. If they continue being upset, let them sit out of the game for two or three minutes before joining in again.
- If a child has hurt himself slightly and lies on the floor pretending to be very hurt, it is usually effective to make him laugh: *Oh dear! We're going to have to take you to hospital and give you a BIG needle! Shall we take you to hospital?* The child will usually get up with a smile. Of course, be sympathetic and concerned when a child does hurt himself!

Dips

Before playing a game, you may like to choose who is 'it' by using a 'dip', or short action rhyme. Here are two examples. (Stressed syllables are marked with a $^{\prime}$).

One potato

$^{\prime}$*One potato,* $^{\prime}$*two potatoes,* $^{\prime}$*three potatoes,* $^{\prime}$*four,*

$^{\prime}$*Five potatoes,* $^{\prime}$*six potatoes,* $^{\prime}$*seven potatoes,* $^{\prime}$*more!*

- The children form a circle and put a fist out in front of them.
- You (or a pupil) stand in the middle of the circle.
- On each **number** of the rhyme, which everybody says with you, touch a pupil's fist with your own fist. Go around the circle and touch a different fist each time, finishing with the word *more*.
- The pupil who is touched on the word *more* is either out (and you continue the dip until there is one pupil left, who becomes 'it'), or becomes 'it'.

Hippy, hipperdation

– Hippy, – hipper – da – tion,

– How – many – people – are – at – the – sta – tion?

This is another rhyme to be used in the same way as 'One potato'.

- On each word or syllable within dashes, touch a different fist.
- The child whose fist is touched on the last syllable of *station*, says a number, e.g. *six*. Count six fists from this child and the owner of fist 6, is 'it'.

Think of a similar rhyme in L1 that your class might use in the same way. This will help them to understand what you are doing and to realise that children in other countries do many of the same things.

Games to play outside the classroom

1 Run, run!

This game is an excellent way to teach action verbs, adverbs and lexical sets, and to work on sound discrimination. You can use it for five minutes every day, right from the start, and develop it. Use it when a class needs livening up or as part of the class routine.

Playing the game

1 Basic procedure

- Take the children somewhere where they have some space and simply give out orders which the children have to follow.
- Shout *Run, run, run!* to get them started.
- Do each action with them and use voice inflection.
- When they seem to recognise each order (after a few lessons), only use voice inflection and finally, only give the order.
- At the beginning, say each verb three times; eventually, say it only once to train your pupils to listen and recognise the different verbs.
- After each new order, say *Stop!* and clap your hands (this is to save your voice). The children have to stop suddenly and stand completely still in whatever position they are in. Then give the next order. *Walk, walk, walk!* ... *Stop!* ... *Jump, jump, jump!* ... *Stop!* etc.

Think of what children do. What action verbs would be the most useful to teach so that a child can talk about himself, his activities and his surroundings? Make a list of these verbs. Which ones could you use with 'Run, run!'? Compare your list with the one in part 3 below. Add any verbs that you think are useful.

2 Extensions

- Children love it if they are 'out' if they move after you say *Stop!* Before you play it like this, however, have a quick practice session. That way, all the children have the chance to hear the verbs again before they start being eliminated.
- Children who are 'out' help you to shout out the orders or they play the role of 'teacher'.
- Add adverbs or adverbial phrases to the orders, e.g. *Walk quickly!/ slowly!/ with giant steps!/ heavily!*
- Use nouns after the verbs, e.g. *Ride a bike! Eat a hamburger!*
- Give orders which use words that sound similar to those in L1. The children have to guess the meaning. e.g. *Play the piano! Play football!*
- Use verbs that sound the same to develop the ear, e.g. *Sing! Swing! Swim!*
- Use the negative, e.g. *Dance! ... Don't dance, play football!*
- Use it to practise the present continuous. e.g.
  T: *Climb a tree! ... Stop! ... What are you doing?*
  Class: *We're climbing!*

3 Useful verbs to teach

run	*drink*
walk	*throw a ball*
jump	*catch a ball*
play (a sport)	*kick*
play (an instrument)	*climb*
ride a bike	*dance*
watch TV	*sing*
eat	*swim*
swing	*fly*
fight	*skate*
shout	*push*

2 Go to …

This game is good for practising vocabulary and some basic questions such as *Where are you going?*, *Where are you?* and *Where did you go?* It also gives those children who are relatively weak at English, but who run well, a chance to win.

Playing the game

1 Basic procedure

- Teach or revise the vocabulary you want to use (e.g. the rooms of the house, shops, places). The following steps explain why and how you will use the vocabulary.
- Go somewhere where there is some space.
- Choose 3–5 different places within that space (e.g. a corner, a wall, a tree, or just some boxes chalked on the ground).
- Decide what you want to call each place, and tell the class.
- Then get the pupils to point to each place in answer to your questions. e.g. *Where is the kitchen?*
- Then have a trial run. Say *Go to the bedroom!* and point to it.
- Eliminate the last child or the last two or three children to get to the place or any child who has run to the wrong place. The last two or three children left in the group are the winners. (*Linda, Danny and Robert are the winners!*)

2 Extensions

- Point in the wrong direction to make the children listen more carefully.
- Add adjectives to the places, e.g. *Run to the big house! Run to the blue tree!* (Put a blue circle on the tree beforehand.)
- Change the verbs, e.g. *run, hop, fly to …*
- Get the whole class to ask a specific question before you tell them where to go.
  Class: *Where are you going?*
  T: *I'm going to Grandma's house!*
  (Everybody runs to 'Grandma's house'.)
- Children who are 'out', shout out the places with you or take your place.

Adaptations for younger children

Get the children to mime an action when they get to the place. e.g. they can sleep in the bedroom, or wash their hands in the bathroom.

3 Red light, green light

This game is suitable for the beginning of the year as a way of getting to know your pupils' names, getting them to follow a few basic instructions and to say their names.

Playing the game

1 Basic procedure

- Get your pupils to stand in a line one beside the other, facing you. You are about 30 m away from them.

- Turn around to face a wall or tree ('home'), so your back is facing the children. Call out *One, two, three, stop!*
- In the meantime, the children run towards you, trying to get as close to you as possible. When you say *stop!* they have to stop and stay completely still.
- As soon as you say *stop!*, turn quickly around and see if anyone is moving.
- If someone does move, ask *What's your name?*
  Pupil: *My name's Geraldine.*
  T: *Go back, Geraldine!*
  And Geraldine has to go back to the starting line.
- Turn around to face the wall again and repeat the procedure. The game finishes when a pupil touches 'home' before you see him. That pupil then takes your place while you help him with the new language involved.

2 Extensions

- Make the number sequence longer or change it. e.g. *One, two, three* the first time, *four, five, six* the second, etc.
- Change your question. e.g. *How are you? What colour are your shoes?*

4 Crocodile

This game teaches the use of *can* and *can't* for asking for, granting and refusing permission, *I am/we are*, action verbs, the construction of longer and longer sentences, and a range of vocabulary.

Playing the game

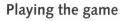

I am a crocodile!

1 Basic procedure

- Divide the children into two groups and get each group into a line, facing each other and standing about 40 m apart.
- Stand between the two lines. You are the crocodile, so stretch out your arms, one above the other and with palms facing each other, so your arms are like a crocodile's big mouth.
- Clap your palms together, chanting rhythmically *I - AM - A - CROCODILE!*
- The children have to ask *Can I go?* The crocodile answers either *Yes, you can!* or *No, you can't!*, in which case they have to ask permission to pass again.
- When the crocodile says *Yes, you can*, the children have to try and run past him to the opposite side (exchanging places with the other group), without getting caught.
- Whoever gets caught by the crocodile, becomes a crocodile and has to help catch the others. (*Geraldine and John are crocodiles!*) All the crocodiles make crocodile mouths with their arms and chant with you *We are crocodiles! We are crocodiles!* The other children ask permission to go again and the game continues until there are only two children left. They are the winners. (*Jessica and Teresa are the winners!*)

2 Extensions

- Get the children to ask permission to go somewhere specific. e.g. *Can I go to the beach?/the restaurant?/the park?* (You can show a picture of a beach, etc. to prompt them.)

- Make them ask permission using longer and longer sentences. e.g. *Can I go to the park? Can I go to the park with Louise? Can I go to the park with Louise and Armand?*
- The crocodile mimes an action and the children have to ask permission accordingly. e.g. *Can I fly?/swim?/run?*
- In your answers, mention methods of transport. e.g.
  Class: *Can I/we go?*
  T: *Yes. You can go by train.*

  The children run past pretending they are trains.

  Or prompt them with an action to ask *Can we go by train?*
  T: *No, you can't.*
  Class: *Can we go by bicycle?*
  T: *Yes, you can.*

Adaptation for older children

Answer their question with *Yes, but only if you have blue jeans/brown hair/long hair*, etc.

5 It's your ball

This game is useful for teaching the apostrophe *s* for possession (*Louise's*), *his/her* and *my/your*.

Teacher preparation

Equipment needed: a large ball, a beanbag or a pair of rolled-up socks.

Playing the game

1 Basic procedure

- Very young children find it very difficult to catch a ball, so get them to sit in a circle with their legs spread out and roll a big ball to each other.
- For older children, use a beanbag or a pair of rolled-up socks to throw to each other. Don't use a ball because balls bounce and can roll away from your playing area, breaking the rhythm of the game.
- The players simply roll the ball or throw the beanbag to each other, saying the name of the person they are sending it to: *It's Luc's ball*. If the pupil who sent the ball or beanbag does not say the apostrophe *s* at the end of the name, or gets the name wrong, he has to stand in the middle of the circle until he hears another pupil make a mistake. Then he takes this pupil's place.

2 Extensions

- The children say *his/her ball*, depending on whether they are sending it to a boy or a girl.
- One child throws the ball to another child, saying *It's your ball*. The second child says, on catching the ball *It's my ball*, and then throws it to a third child, saying *It's your ball* and so on.

6 Whose is it?

This game practises the questions *Whose (hand) is it? Whose (shoes) are they?* and the apostrophe *s* for possession.

Teacher preparation

Equipment needed: a sheet and a washing line. ◆ SEE PAGE 10

Playing the game

1 Basic procedure

- Hang a sheet on a washing line and make a few pupils go behind it.
- Get them to lift their arms up, one after the other, so that the other children, in front of the sheet, can only see their hands.

  T: *Whose hand is it?* (The class can ask this with you.)

  Class: *It's Maria's/Juan's/Linda's hand!*

- When a pupil guesses correctly, he takes the place of the person who held up his hand.

2 Extensions

- Ask *Whose shoes* (or even *feet*, if you are willing to let the children take off their shoes and socks) *are they?*
- Draw some funny faces on the sheet and cut out a little hole where the nose should be. The children behind the sheet fit their noses into the different holes and the question then becomes *Whose nose is it?*

7 There are three in your group

This game is good for teaching or practising *there is/there are* and numbers.

Playing the game

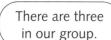

Basic procedure

- Get the children to walk around, and then suddenly say *There are (three) in your group!*
- The children have to quickly get into groups of (three).
- Go to each group and ask how many there are in their group. Each group has to answer. *There are (three) in our group.*
- Any children who are not in a group of (three), are 'out'.
- When you see that there may be trouble because there are too many in the group and no one wants to leave, just say *There is one in your group* so that everyone separates to become a 'group' of one.
- Repeat until there are only two or three students left.

Games to play inside the classroom

1 Touch something

This game is good for teaching colours, certain adjectives and other lexical sets.

Teacher preparation

Put some drawings up in different parts of the classroom.

Playing the game

1 Basic procedure

- Call out the name of what is in one of the drawings you have put up, e.g. a house. The children run and stand under this picture. (If you prefer a quieter class, they can sit at their desks and point at the picture you are referring to.)

2 Extensions

- If you are teaching colours, do not just put a colour on the wall but a picture of an object in different colours, e.g. a blue house, a red house, a green ball and an orange ball. The object is not important, but you are teaching the children to put the adjective in front of the noun. There will come a time when this will 'sound right' and they will use this word order naturally.
- Use whatever you have in the classroom. e.g. a blue sweater, a big chair.
- Use the game to teach definite and indefinite articles. e.g. *Touch the floor/the door/a chair/a window*, etc.

2 The number game

This game is useful for teaching and revising numbers, or any kind of series (the days of the week, months of the year, etc. for older children). It is also good for developing the automatic use of this language.

Playing the game

1 Basic procedure

- Say the first number in a series (*One*) and point to a child in the class who has to say *Two*. Then point to another who has to say *Three*, etc.
- Do this more and more quickly until somebody makes a mistake or doesn't answer quickly enough. That pupil is 'out'. Everybody says *You – are – out!*
- Continue until there are only one or two pupils left. Of course, the pupils who are 'out' can also shout *You – are – out!* when somebody makes a mistake. That way nobody takes it personally and, at the same time, everybody is paying attention to the game. You are also practising *you are*.
- Help slower children by mouthing the beginning of the word while you stand in front of them or by giving them the beginning sound. However don't make it into a habit or they will learn to depend on your signal.

2 Extensions

- You can do the same with slightly older children to drill them. Instead of pointing at a child, throw a pair of socks for him to catch, saying *One*. He catches the socks, says *Two* and throws them to another child who says *Three*, etc. (As explained above, it is best to use a pair of rolled-up socks or a beanbag since a ball will bounce all over the classroom and interrupt the rhythm of the game.)

- Give the class two or three categories of nouns, e.g. land, sea, air or colours and clothes. Throw the socks to a child and say *Colour!* The child says a colour (e.g. *Red!*) and throws the socks back to you. Throw them to another child and say *Clothes!* He answers with the name of a garment. (e.g. *Sweater!*)

- You may or may not eliminate a child if he makes a mistake.

- Use this game for questions and answers such as *Where can I buy flowers? At the flower shop.*, etc.

3 Thumbs up!

This game is good for differentiating between *is* and *has got* which young (and older!) children seem to confuse. It practises names for the parts of the body, colours and clothes and helps children to start making descriptions. It is also good for differentiating between *he* and *she*.

Playing the game

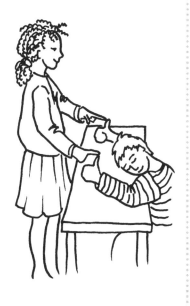

1 Basic procedure

- Choose a certain number of children who go to the front of the class.

- The others put their heads down on their desks, close their eyes and put their fists on the desk, with each thumb up.

- The children standing at the front of the class silently go to the other pupils, touch their thumbs and go back to the front of the class.

- If there are a lot more pupils sitting than touching, the 'touchers' can touch more than one pupil so that everyone gets touched.

- The 'touchers' then go back to the front of the class and stand in a line facing the others.

- When you give the signal, the pupils at their desks open their eyes. One by one, they have to guess who touched them. They do this by describing them. e.g. *She is a girl. She has got a blue sweater.*

- When everybody has described the person they think touched them, ask the 'touchers' *Who did you touch?* They answer *I touched Helena and Bruno. I touched Martin.*

- If a pupil has guessed correctly, he goes to the front of the class and takes the place of the pupil who touched him.

2 Extensions

- Ask the pupils for longer descriptions. e.g. *She is the girl with the blue sweater.* or *She is a pretty girl. She has got brown eyes, long hair and a blue sweater.*

- Ask the pupils to use prepositions in their descriptions. e.g. *She is a girl. She is next to Martin. She has got a blue sweater.*

4 How many fingers ...?

This game is useful for teaching *How many ...?*, for reinforcing *have got* or *there is/there are* and for practising numbers 1–5.

Playing the game

Basic procedure

- Play this game with the class before getting them to play in pairs.
- Ask a child to put his hand behind his back with either one, two, three, four or five fingers out.
  - T: *How many fingers have you got?/How many fingers are there?*
  - P: *Guess!*
  - T: *You've got three fingers./There are three fingers.*
  - P: *No!*
  - T: *You've got one finger!/There is one finger.*
  - P: *Yes, I have!/Yes, there is!*
- The person who is guessing is allowed three guesses. If he has not guessed correctly after these three guesses, he changes places with the other person.
- Teacher and pupil exchange roles and start again.
- Now get the class to play the game in pairs.

Adaptation for older children

Older children (who like competition) can score a point every time they guess correctly. The one with the most points, wins.

5 Writing on backs

This game is useful for practising vocabulary, the letters of the alphabet, spelling short words (for older children) and/or listening to and giving orders.

Playing the game

1 Basic procedure

- Ask the children to stand in a circle, one behind the other so that each child is looking at the back of another. Each child 'writes' a number or letter, or 'draws' a simple picture on the back of the pupil in front of him, using just his finger.
- Each child guesses what was written or drawn on his back. e.g. *It's number five. It's a house.*

2 Extension

- Make the game into a chain activity in which a whole picture (e.g. a face or monster) is drawn on the board.
- Stand the children in a line, with the front of the line near the board.
- The pupil furthest from the board (pupil 1) draws a circle on the back of the child in front of him (pupil 2). Pupil 2 says to the pupil at the front of the line, nearest the board *Draw a circle*. This pupil obeys by drawing a circle on the board.
- Pupil 2 then draws another part of the face (e.g. three eyes) on the back of the pupil in front of him (pupil 3). Pupil 3 says *Draw three eyes* and the pupil nearest the board obeys. This continues until the picture is finished.

6 Beetle

This game is useful for practising *have/haven't got*, the parts of the body, the parts of a house/beetle, etc.

Teacher preparation

Draw a picture of what you want to work on, e.g. the body. Divide it into six numbered sections. e.g. *1 the head, 2 the body, 3 an arm, 4 an arm, 5 a leg, and 6 a leg.* ◈ SEE PHOTOCOPIABLE PAGE 3

Equipment needed: enough photocopies of the picture so that there is one for each child; scissors; dice (one for each group).

Playing the game

Basic procedure

- Give out the photocopies.
- Divide the class into groups of four or five and get each child to cut his photocopy into pieces along the lines. The children put their cut-out pieces in front of them on the group's desk.
- Give each group a dice which they take turns to roll. e.g. One child rolls a 3 so he says *I've got an arm* and takes a piece of paper with an arm on. The next pupil rolls a 1 so he says *I've got a head* and takes a piece with a head on.
- If a pupil rolls the dice and gets a part of the body that he already has, then he has to pass the dice on to the next pupil and cannot take anything.
- The first pupil to complete his 'puzzle' is the winner.

7 Snapdragon

Aims of the game

With a 'snapdragon' (this object has lots of different names) you can practise the questions *What colour do you want?* and *What number do you want?* as well as colours, numbers and, depending on what you want to teach, *you've got, you're* or *you're going to*.

Teacher preparation

Equipment needed: a piece of paper for each child (either A4 size or a square of approximately 21 cm x 21 cm) or copies of PHOTOCOPIABLE PAGE 4; different coloured crayons, pens or pencils.

Playing the game

1 Basic procedure

Making the snapdragon

- Children aged five and upwards love to play this game but you will have to help five-and some six-year-olds to make the snapdragon. You can also ask the children who can make them to help those who cannot.
- Give each child a piece of paper. Get the children to make their pieces into squares or simply give them squares. Tell them to follow your instructions and watch you.
- Take your own square. Fold the square diagonally and make a triangle.
- Take the triangle and fold it into a smaller triangle. Tell the children to hold it up and ask *Like this?*

- Open up the piece of paper. The square should have a fold mark on each diagonal.

A

B

- Take each of the the four corners of the square and take them to the middle. You now have another, smaller square.
- Turn this square over and repeat the process by taking each corner of this square to the middle. Your snapdragon is now finished.
- While the children are busy, quickly make a couple of extra ones for the children who do not manage to make one.
- Tell the children to put the numbers 1–8 on each triangle of side A and a colour on each square of side B.
- Get the children to lift the triangles (where the numbers are) and draw an object, animal or person in each triangle under the number.
- With the side with triangles facing you (side A), fold the snapdragon in half, inwards towards the middle. Slip the thumb and index finger of each hand under the flaps formed by the squares on side B. Bring your thumbs towards you, and move your index fingers away from you, thus making the snapdragon move.
- Bring your thumbs and index fingers together again and this time, move the thumb and index finger of one hand away from the thumb and index finger of the other. Bring them back again and start again. (This process is not at all as complicated as it sounds.)

Using the snapdragon

- Now you are ready to play! Ask a pupil to come to the front of the class and play with you. Move the snapdragon with your fingers. Let your partner see the colours on the snapdragon.
  T: *What colour do you want?*
  P: *Yellow./I want yellow.*
  T: *Yellow.* (T moves the snapdragon twice, once on each syllable of *yellow*.)
- Now open the snapdragon so that the pupil can see the numbers inside.
  T: *What number do you want?*
  P: *Six.*
- Count while making the snapdragon move with each number: *One, two, three, four, five, six!*
- Ask the same questions two more times, and on the last time, open up the snapdragon to show the triangle behind, for example, number 4.
- If there is a picture of a cat under number 4, say *You're a cat!/ You're going to be a cat!/You've got a cat!*, depending on what you want to teach.
- Change places with the other person and then find a new partner. Everybody goes around the class playing with each other.

T A S K

Which of the games above would be most suitable for working on:

1 colours?	6 places?	11 *Whose ...?*
2 parts of the body?	7 classroom objects?	12 *there is/there are?*
3 numbers?	8 possession?	13 *How many ...?*
4 action verbs?	9 *to be?*	
5 clothes?	10 permission?	

◆ SEE KEY PAGE 90 for answers ◆ SEE CHAPTER 6 for other games and activities on some of the same themes.

CHAPTER 6

Vocabulary

In this chapter we look first at how to choose vocabulary to teach and then at how to teach it in interesting and effective ways.

"How do I select vocabulary to teach?"

Before teaching children new vocabulary, it is essential to carefully select the word or words within a particular word group that you want to teach. Here are some things to bear in mind when choosing this vocabulary.

- Remember that there is both active and passive vocabulary. ('Active' vocabulary is what the children both understand and use; 'passive' vocabulary is what they understand but are not able, or required, to use.) Obviously most of the words you use in class will only be passive vocabulary for young children.
- Choose vocabulary that is relevant to your pupils' age, lives and interests. e.g. nationality or telling the time have no meaning for a four-year-old.
- Keep your expectations realistic. Have a basic group of words that you want to teach the whole class, the number of which will depend on their age group. You can teach some extra words to the quicker pupils and the slower ones may absorb them passively, but do not expect the slower ones to use them actively.
- See if there are any words that resemble L1 (*football* is an easy word for most children).
- Think of what they already know which might be easy to build on. e.g. if they know *flower* and *toy* it is easy to teach them *flower shop* and *toy shop* when they are learning names for shops.
- You can expect your pupils to find some word groups more difficult to learn than others, for a number of reasons.
  - … If a word group consists mainly of words of an origin that is unfamiliar to your pupils (e.g. English words of Anglo-Saxon origin are unfamiliar to speakers of Romance languages), then these will be hard to learn.
  - … Words that are difficult to pronounce, or are long, can also be problematic.
  - … Food is usually an easy topic (e.g. *salad, hamburger, spaghetti*), while clothes are quite difficult, with lots of words that sound similar (e.g. *shirt, skirt, shorts*).
- When playing a game with the whole class, take care to choose the right level of vocabulary for each pupil: challenge a quicker pupil with a difficult word and encourage a slower pupil with an easy one.

"How can I teach difficult words?"

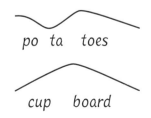

Before teaching a number of new words, check to see which ones will present the most difficulty. Here are some ideas to help you teach them more easily.

- Get the children to clap on the stressed syllable(s) of a word as they say it. e.g. *bi–(clap)–cy–cle*.
- Put the word in a rhythmic or rhyming sentence. e.g. *I eat meat. Rice is nice! I fly through the sky!*
- Separate the word into syllables as you say it, getting the children to follow the sound curve in the air with their fingers. (See diagrams.)
- Teach words that rhyme, together. e.g. *nose* and *toes*.
- Get your pupils to visualise a picture from rhyming words. e.g. *a spoon in the moon*.

• Get the children to repeat a word after you in different ways. e.g. in a deep voice or a little, squeaky voice, in a whisper or a shout, slowly or quickly, etc.

1 Look at this lexical set of classroom objects:

sharpener, pen, ruler, glue, felt tip, pencil, rubber.

Which of the ways of teaching vocabulary suggested above could you use to teach these words? In which order would you teach them? ◆ SEE KEY PAGE 90 for suggested answers.

2 Before your next lesson, look over the vocabulary you want to teach. Which words do you think your pupils will have trouble with? Why? What can you do to help them remember these words? Choose one or two of the above-mentioned techniques and try them out.

Here are some suggestions for how to teach vocabulary in ways that will make it easily understandable to young children, and that will be enjoyable at the same time.

Pictures

Pictures are an obvious, simple and easy way to teach vocabulary. If they are attractive, children will love them. So look out for good pictures all the time, especially in magazines, and keep them for future use. ◆ SEE RESOURCES FOR ACTIVITIES PAGE 10

• Make sure the pictures are simple, clear and can be seen from the back of the class.

• Stick your pictures on coloured card and cover them with transparent adhesive plastic to protect them.

• Choose a different colour for each lexical set. This will help you identify them quickly and the children will also learn to identify lexical sets.

• Write the name of the object in a corner, on the back of the card, so you can show the picture to the class and know what you are showing.

• Enlarge a photocopy to make a poster and use it to teach vocabulary. You can divide a sheet of paper into four and have each part enlarged to A3 size. Tape the sheets together and you will have a good poster. Get active children or those who finish their work quickly to colour it for you.

• Later, give each pupil the same photocopy in its normal size. They can colour it, while you go around checking what they know. Use it as an end-of-unit task or for recording pupils' progress ◆ SEE PAGE 18, or for testing.

• It is a good idea to have two pictures or posters which show the same subject but which are slightly different. Use the first poster to teach the vocabulary and structures. Then use the second one to see if your pupils can use the new language without the visual prompts or reminders of the first poster. This is a good way to find out how much your pupils have assimilated, and is another useful exercise for testing. ◆ SEE PHOTOCOPIABLE PAGES 5 AND 6

Building a paragraph

- When your pupils are older, use pictures to gradually teach them how to build a paragraph. When they see a picture, children usually start by commenting on the first detail that catches their eye. e.g. about a picture of a park, they will say *The flower is red*. Try and teach them to begin by saying what the picture is (*It's a park*), and then to talk about bigger things before going into detail. Get them to finish by saying something general about the picture (*I like the park/the picture*). This sequencing of ideas can be taught by asking questions, e.g. *What's this? What is the most important thing in the picture? Do you like the ...?*

Murals

Murals are excellent teaching materials, especially if the children make them themselves. Making a mural with your pupils is a very complete lesson, though you will need more than one lesson to finish it. Once finished, a mural decorates the class and is a good teaching material.

Making a mural

Example: a town

- Get a big piece of brown paper (the type to wrap big parcels in), about 1 m x 1 m, depending on how many students you have got. The sheet of paper has to be big enough to let the children put all they want on, but not so big as to discourage them because it looks as if it will never be finished.
- Draw two parallel lines across the paper. This is the main street. Now draw a picture of a house on the street.
- Give a sheet of white paper to each child and as you do so ask *What are you going to draw?*
  P: *I'm going to draw a toy shop.*
  T: *OK, draw a toy shop./There are three toy shops. We need a restaurant. Can you/Do you want to draw a restaurant?* etc.
- While each child is drawing, go around asking questions and commenting, e.g. *What are you doing? That's a pretty park. Are there flowers in your park?*
- Have plenty of spare paper for those who need to start again.
- When a child finishes drawing, he comes to you.
  P: *I've finished. Can I colour the restaurant?*
  T: *Yes. Colour the restaurant and then come here.*
- Keep the scissors and the glue so that the children have to ask for them. e.g. *Can I have the scissors, please? Can I cut out the park, please?*
- When the children have finished colouring their pictures they come to you to glue their pictures onto the brown paper.
  P: *Can I glue the park?*
  T: *Where are you going to glue the park?*
  P: *Next to the house.*
  T: *Good. Here is the glue. Just use a little.* etc.
- Keep the quicker children occupied: *We need cars and bicycles. Can you draw a car for the street, please?*

- You can also get the children to cut out pictures from magazines instead of drawing them. Lexical sets like furniture or animals are easy to find. You can combine background drawings and magazine pictures to make a collage. e.g. paint or colour trees, mountains, etc. and glue on pictures of animals.
- Use the mural to decorate the class. The children will be proud to see their work on the wall.
- Use it as a poster. e.g.:
  T: *What's this?*
  P: *It's a school.*
  T: *Where is the school?*
  P: *Next to the house.*
  T: *Whose toyshop is it?*
  P: *It's Paula's toyshop.*
  T: *What colour is Ben's shoe shop? How many ...? Do you like ...? Where is the biggest park? etc.*

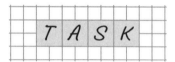

Which lexical sets do you think would make the best murals? Try using making a mural to illustrate one of these sets.

Crafts

An excellent way to teach a language is through activities, e.g. making crafts, making a sandwich, laying a table, planting a seed, studying an insect. These are all interesting, authentic activities that involve children as well as teach them English. Older children who are learning to write can keep a simple diary of their activities, with two or three lines of description and a drawing of the activity.

A potato man

A fun and easy craft is making a potato man (or animal).

Teacher preparation

Materials needed: one potato per child (and a few extras, just in case), toothpicks for the arms and legs, wool for the hair (have two or three different colours), felt tip pens for drawing the face, scissors, and, for older children, some card for making hands, shoes, etc. and some tape to fasten these to the toothpicks.

Making the craft

1 Basic procedure

- Revise the names for parts of the body and teach the words you are going to need for the craft.
- Demonstrate and explain in English how to make the potato man and keep the wool, extra toothpicks, tape and card on your table so the children have to come and ask you for them in English.
- Give out the potatoes. Each child asks *Can I have a potato, please?* Give each child only two or three toothpicks so they have to come and ask for more.
- They stick the toothpicks into the potato, some for his arms and legs, and some on his head. They can they wind the wool round the sticks to look like hair. They draw his face.

- Here are some expressions they will need:

Can I have … , please? *Come here, please.*   *I haven't got (the scissors).*

Can I have more …? *I need (three toothpicks).*   *Where is/are (the scissors)?*

Can you help me …? *I need more (yellow wool).* *I can't (cut it).*

I want (some blue wool), please. I don't want red. (Offer the wrong colour wool to your pupil on purpose, so that he has to use verbs like *I don't want, I don't like*.)

2 Extension

- Later, they can draw a picture of their potato man and while they are drawing, you can go around the class and get them to describe their man to you.

Adaptation for older children

Ask the children to write a line or two and/or invent a little dialogue in pairs, using their potato men. (e.g. *Hello! How are you? What's your name? Do you like sweets?* etc.)

Sequences

A sequence is a series of short, repetitive sentences that form a cohesive whole. Put the vocabulary you want to teach into these sentences.

Depending on the verbs you use, you can make the sequence into a little play.

◈ SEE PAGE 63

Example: Take a crayon

Take a crayon. (Pretend to take a crayon in the air in front of you. Later, when the children know the sequence, you can ask them *What colour are you going to take/choose?*)

Draw a picture. (Pretend to draw a picture in the air in front of you.)

Colour the picture. (Pretend to colour the picture.)

Show the picture to the class. (Pretend to turn the picture around so that everyone can see it.)

It's beautiful! (Give a big clap and show great enthusiasm.)

- Say the sequence and the children listen.
- Say it again, and this time the children do the actions with you.
- Say it again, and the children repeat each sentence after you, as well as doing the actions.
- Finally, the children say the sequence with you, doing all the actions.

Stories

An enjoyable way to teach vocabulary to children is to make it into a story which you can illustrate on the board with pictures, drawings and/or with actions. You can do this over a number of lessons. Here are some tips on how to do this, and an example.

- Young children do not need complicated stories: on the contrary, the simpler the better.

- Tell part of the story with drawings, then stop and repeat it. Help them say the new words.
- Keep the children's attention by illustrating as you go along so they are eager to see what is coming next.
- Be sure to put in some known vocabulary too, to give them confidence. Then add on the next part. Your children will normally get so involved in the story that they will forget that they are using English and want more.
- Continue with the story over a number of lessons, starting each time from the beginning.
- If you have drawn pictures on the board, point to them and get the class to tell you the story.
- Ask a child to draw the story as you or another child tells it.
- When the children know the story, get them to draw it in their notebooks, and while they are drawing, go around the class and get individual pupils to tell you the story.
- Draw parts of the story in a different order and get the children to say the corresponding sentences or express the ideas.
- Do not worry about your artistic abilities. Children think anything a teacher draws is great and at the most, they will have a good laugh and associate what you have drawn with what it is supposed to be.

Example: nature vocabulary

(target vocabulary: *tree, forest, sky, sun, moon, star, mountain, river*)

This is the witch. (Draw.)

The witch lives in a tree. (Draw.)

The witch lives in a tree (point) *in the forest.* (Draw two or three trees. Encourage the children to say *tree*, and the other new words, when you point to the pictures.) *The witch lives in a tree* (point), *in the forest* (point), *in the mountains.* (Draw.)

The witch is HUNGRY! (Rub your stomach and mime hunger.)

She's going to fly (mime) *through the sky* (point). *She's going to fly* (mime) *through the sky* (point) *and visit the stars* (draw), *the moon* (draw) *and the sun* (draw).

Some children live in a house (draw) *beside a river* (draw). *Here is the house. Here is the river. Here are the children!* (Draw a face in the window of the house.)

The witch is hungry (mime). *She's going to eat* (mime) *the children!*

A bear (draw) *lives in the mountains. The bear likes the children.*

Here is the witch. She's going to eat the children. The children see (mime) *the witch. Help! Help!* (The children cry out *Help! Help!* and mime with you.)

The bear (point) *runs and catches* (mime both actions) *the witch. He throws the witch into the river* (mime and point to river). *Goodbye, witch!* (The children say goodbye with you and wave.)

Stories with pupils in them

If you tell a story or do some drawings with your pupils in them, you will be sure to have your pupils' complete attention.

Example

Here is the sea (draw some wavy lines). *Here is Glenda.* (Glenda has got long hair, so draw a little circle with a smile, a nose, eyes and lots of long hair.) *Glenda is swimming. She is swimming in the sea. Here is Ben.* (Ben has glasses.) *He is in the boat.* (Draw a simple sailing boat, and in it, a face with glasses.) *Glenda and Ben are happy.* etc.

- After you have taught the vocabulary this way, start asking questions. e.g. *Where is Ben? What is Glenda doing?*
- The children can then retell the story.
- If you find it difficult to create your own stories, most publishers sell readers for beginners that are easy to adapt.

Picture dictations

In a picture dictation, children simply listen carefully and draw what you tell them. It is an excellent activity for developing listening and comprehension skills, as well as a useful way of evaluating your pupils' understanding. The dictations should get more complicated as the school year progresses.

Example: 'My friend'

- Give each pupil a copy of the outline of a body.  SEE PHOTOCOPIABLE PAGE 7 Giving them an outline helps them draw things around or on it, and avoids problems of them running out of space on their piece of paper (young children do not have a sense of proportion).
- Warn your pupils that 'your friend' is very different, partly so that they will listen carefully, but mainly so that they will actually draw what you are saying, and not what they think is correct. Many children just will not accept a person with four eyes and will draw 'your friend' with two, even though they have understood what you have said.
- Begin *My friend has got four eyes. He has got four yellow eyes*, etc. Be sure to make the instructions unusual. (So many picture dictations say things like *Colour the water blue!*)
- Be patient and give your pupils time to draw, but remind them it is not a drawing competition.

- At the end of the dictation, you can ask your pupils to find a name for 'your friend'. Ask them what he eats, where he lives or anything else related to what you have already taught.
- Correct the dictation by drawing the outline on the board and asking some pupils to describe your friend again while others go to the board and draw.

Adaptation for older children

This activity can be played as a communication game, in pairs, as follows.

- Each child has a sheet of paper which he divides into two halves with a line.
- Each child draws a monster in one half. Pupil 1 describes his monster to pupil 2, while pupil 2 draws what pupil 1 says in the blank half of paper.
- They exchange roles and then compare their drawings.

Videos

Young children like watching videos but only in short sessions, otherwise they get bored.

- Teach the main new vocabulary items before you show the video. That way children understand or at least catch words or phrases so they:

  … are encouraged to listen

  … get the satisfaction of seeing that they can understand something.

- Stop the video (use the 'pause' button) after an example of some new language and ask *What did (he) say?* If they cannot repeat what was said, rewind the tape and get them to listen again.
- Stop the video at an interesting scene and ask *What's that? Where's …? How many …?*
- Stop the video and ask *What's going to happen? What did he do? What's he going to do? What's he doing?* to use different tenses. Silent videos like the BBC series *Pingu* are especially good for this, as the children can concentrate more on the story which is very simple.
- With videos that actually teach, ask the children to play the part of the learner. (The BBC's *Muzzy* is excellent, although only episodes 1-6 are really easy enough for young learners.)
- After showing the video, describe a character and ask the children to guess who he is. e.g. *He's bad. He's got a long nose. He's clever.* (Corvax from *Muzzy*.)
- Get the children to draw a picture from the video and tell you or the class about it.
- Play the same video often. Children must learn to hear and the more they listen to a video, the more they will understand.

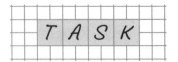

There are many ways you can use a video to teach language. Can you think of an activity that is not mentioned above? Compare and share your ideas with other teachers.

Card games

Cards with pictures are extremely versatile and can be used in many games which are very popular with children.

Getting the children to make their own picture cards makes an excellent lesson and saves you time, too. Here are some tips on how to make and look after picture cards, and then some games which use the cards to teach vocabulary. For useful language ◆ SEE PHOTOCOPIABLE PAGE 2

Making cards

- For some games, the children will need a set of cards each, so simply give them a copy of PHOTOCOPIABLE PAGES 8–10 which they cut out, using the procedure explained below.

- For other games, you will only need a set for every 6–8 children. These should be glued onto card or cheap playing cards. Children seem to think that they are 'really' playing if the pictures are glued onto real playing cards.

- Remember that young children have trouble managing scissors and can get upset if the picture that they have cut out is not well cut. Make it easier for them by drawing the pictures in squares of dotted lines so they can cut along those lines.

Materials needed: photocopies (one for each child) of the pictures of the vocabulary you have taught. If you want to stick them onto coloured card, give out squares of it. (It is a good idea to choose a specific colour for each category of cards.) Extra copies for children who need to start again.

- Revise the vocabulary with them.

Basic procedure

- Start the cutting-out.
  - T: *What are we going to cut out?*
  - P1: *Shoes!*
  - T: *No, we're not going to cut out shoes.*
  - P2: *A sweater!*
  - T: *Yes. We're going to cut out a sweater. Show me the sweater. Good. Now, cut out the sweater. Glue the sweater to the yellow card. Good. Now what are we going to cut out?* etc.

- While they are cutting out, you can go around asking *What are you doing? What's that?*

- Remember, your children are young and need time to cut out and glue. (Use a glue stick, not paste, with your pupils under six.)

- If the pictures are glued onto card, it will be worth your while to cover them in transparent sticky plastic as children have a great tendency to bite or twist the cards in excitement. However, if covered in plastic, the cards can last several years.

Looking after cards

- Once the cards have been made, give each child an envelope labelled with a 'category' (e.g. *food*, *clothes*) and an appropriate drawing.

- Each child puts his cards in the envelope and then gives the envelope to you. Keep all the envelopes in a box so that you can look after them and use them with other classes.

- When the children are putting their cards away, remind them to look under the table, etc. to see that no cards are lost.
- Occasionally you should use a lesson to check the contents fo the envelopes and complete them if necessary. This is a good way of revising vocabulary. (*Who's got a shop? I haven't got a shop! I've got two shops! Give a shop to David, then.*)

1 Who has ...?

Teacher preparation

Materials needed: a card for each child.

Playing the game

Basic procedure

- Give each child a card and say *Who has a sweater?* or *Show me a sweater*. The children with sweater cards hold them up. Say *Good. Now, who has got shoes?* etc.
- After a while, the children exchange cards and start again.

2 Show me

Teacher preparation

Materials needed: an envelope of cards for each child, and one for yourself.

Playing the game

1 Basic procedure

- Get the children to place all their cards in front of them on the desk, face up. Say *Show me ... shoes!* The children find the shoes as quickly as they can and hold them up. Continue like this.

2 Extension

- Work on sound discrimination by asking them to show you cards of words that they tend to confuse. e.g. *a skirt*, then *a shirt*, then *shoes*.

Adaptation for older children

- Make things more difficult by asking them to show you two objects. e.g. *Show me shoes and jeans*. This will oblige them to listen to longer sentences.

3 Bingo

Young children love bingo as long as it does not take too long. This version is very quick to play.

Teacher preparation

Materials needed: the envelopes of the cards for the category of vocabulary you want to practise – one for each child.

Playing the game

1 Basic procedure

- Give each child an envelope, and keep one for yourself.
- Get the children to choose three cards from their envelopes and put them in front of them on the table, face up.
- Take a card at random out of your own envelope.
- Depending on what you want to teach, ask a useful question. If you are teaching food vocabulary and you pick out a 'sandwich', you could ask *Do you like sandwiches?*
- The children who have a card of a sandwich, hold it up and say *Yes, I like sandwiches*. They then put this card face down on the table.
- If nobody has got a 'sandwich' card, the whole class says *Nobody likes sandwiches!* or *I don't like sandwiches.*
- Continue asking until someone has turned over all three of their cards and says *Bingo!* The prize can be that the winner gets to call out the following game.

2 Extensions

- To practise language for places, try this:

  Class: *Where are you?/Where are you going?/Where did you go?*

  T: *I'm in ...* (takes a card out of the envelope) *the restaurant!*

  P: *I'm in the restaurant, too!*
- To practise language for clothes, the class can ask *What are you wearing?/What are you going to put on?* etc.

4 Memory

Teacher preparation

Materials needed: about 20 cards for each group of eight children.

Playing the game

1 Preparation

You will have to teach younger children how to play first.

- Sit them in a circle with the cards in the middle, face down.
- Explain to the children that they have to find two cards with the same picture to make a pair. They can only turn over two cards.
- If they make a pair, they can have another turn. If they don't, they miss a turn.
- The person with the most pairs is the winner.

2 Basic procedure

- You can play this game in groups of eight, with four teams of two that play against each other.
- The first member of team 1 turns over a card (e.g. a picture of a ball).
- The whole group asks *Have you got a ball?* The second member of the first team turns over another card and says *Yes, we have* or *No, we haven't.*
- If team 1 finds the pair, they say *It's our turn again.* If they do not find it, team 2 says *It's our turn.*

- To practise words for places, the group can ask *Where are you going?/Where are you?* etc. The answer can be *I'm going to the toy shop*, etc.

Adaptation for older children

- Use action cards to practise tenses. The group ask *What are you doing?/What are you going to do?* etc.
- The first member of team 1 turns over a card and says, e.g. *I'm playing tennis*. The second member turns over another card, hoping to find the pair, and says *I'm playing tennis, too* or *I'm not playing tennis*.

5 Grids

Teacher preparation

Materials needed: a copy of a grid ◆ SEE PHOTOCOPIABLE PAGE 11 for each child, one or two envelopes of cards for each child.

Playing the game

Basic procedure

- Give each child a grid with numbers and an envelope of cards.
- Get them to put their cards face up on the table.
- Say *Number 3 is a train*. The children find the train and put it on number 3. Then say *Number 1 is a bicycle*. The children put the bicycle on number 1, etc.
- Check to see that everyone has properly completed their grids.
- When one grid is finished, get the children to put away the remaining cards (e.g. all the left-over vehicles) into the envelope for that category and hand out the envelopes for another category, e.g. furniture envelopes. Then start again *Put the sofa on the train*, etc.
- Once the children can play with you, get them to try playing in pairs.

6 Spin

Teacher preparation

Materials needed: 12 cards and a pencil.

Playing the game

Basic procedure

- Place the cards face up on the table, as though they were the numbers of the clock.
- Put a pencil in the middle of the circle and ask a pupil to spin it. The pencil will stop at a certain card.
- The pupil has to say what the picture is. If he does, he gets a point or gets to spin again. Then it is the next pupil's turn.

Games with pictures, objects and words

Finally, here are some more simple games which require very little preparation but which are fun and stimulating for the children.

1 What's in the bag?

Teacher preparation

Materials needed: several objects and a large bag.

Playing the game

Basic procedure

- Ask each child to come to you, and put his hand into the bag without looking into it (he can close his eyes if he likes). He feels the object and then says what it is.
- The child then takes the object out of the bag and sees if he has guessed correctly.
- If he has, he can take the object back to his seat.

2 Yes and no chairs

Teacher preparation

Materials needed: pictures to stick on the board, two chairs.

Playing the game

Basic procedure

- Draw or put several pictures on the board.
- Place two chairs in front of the board. One is the 'yes' chair and the other the 'no' chair.
- Get the children to stand in two lines, facing the board, with the front of each line nearest the board, about 10 m away from it.
- Point to a picture and say *This is a house!* The first child in each line has to run and try to sit on the 'yes' chair (if you are pointing at a house), or the 'no' one if you are not. The first pupil on the right chair gets a point for his team.

3 Kim's game

Teacher preparation

Materials needed: a number of pictures or real objects.

Playing the game

Basic procedure

- Put some pictures on the board or objects on the table and give the children a few minutes to memorise them. Then ask them to close their eyes.
- Remove or change the position of the pictures/objects. The children tell you the differences they notice.
- The children can play in groups at first, and then as individuals.

4 In my bag there is ...

This game is good for listening and the repetition of a structure, as well as vocabulary practice.

Playing the game

1 Basic procedure

- Say, e.g. *In my bag there is a dog.*
- A pupil repeats this last sentence and adds another object. e.g. *In my bag there is a dog and a cat.*
- Another pupil repeats this last sentence and adds another object. e.g. *In my bag there is a dog, a cat and a book.*
- Only let the children use one or two categories. e.g. animals and school things.

2 Extensions

- Use as many different beginnings as you like, e.g. *I want a dog. I'm playing football. I like pizza and sweaters.*
- Give each child an envelope of cards and ask him to say the object he has drawn from the envelope in his sentence. Later, if someone does not remember the object when they are saying the sentence, the class can prompt him by showing him their card.
- Pupils can help someone who does not remember a word in the sentence by miming the object, by making the sound of the animal in question or by giving a clue in English.

Which of all the games above (with or without cards) would be most suitable for:

1 colours?	5 classroom objects?
2 parts of the body?	6 rooms of the house and furniture?
3 clothes?	7 places?
4 action verbs?	8 animals?

◆ SEE KEY PAGE 91 for answers. ◆ SEE CHAPTERS 5 and 7 for other games and activities on some of these themes.

CHAPTER 7

Rhymes, songs and drama

The ways of teaching young children a language are basically:

… speaking to them

… playing simple games

… providing art and craft activities

… teaching them songs and rhymes

… organising simple drama activities.

Think of as many reasons as you can for using rhymes and songs with young children. Cover the list below. Then compare your answers with the list.

Why use rhymes and songs?

Rhymes and songs are fundamental tools for teaching young children a language for the following reasons:

- They develop the ear which is the first, and one of the most important steps, in learning a language.
- They teach pronunciation, intonation and stress in a natural way.
- They teach vocabulary and structures.
- Most songs and rhymes use repetitive language and/or some set phrases with different words added in particular places.
- Rhymes and songs are a good way of giving children a complete text with meaning, right from the beginning.
- They are always well accepted by children and they are fun. Children enjoy the rhyming sounds and also the strong rhythm used in most rhymes and songs. Children love anything rhythmic and/or musical, and because they enjoy it they assimiliate it easily and quickly.
- They make the children feel close to one another.
- If a child likes a song, he will often sing it by himself, over and over again, outside the English lesson.
- Children of all language abilities can join in, which helps build confidence.
- Children do not need to see the words to learn them.
- Children have met much of their L1 through traditional rhymes.

"How can I use rhymes and songs?"

- Use rhymes and songs to introduce or practise new language. Select them carefully.
- Get children to recite or sing a few songs and rhymes to make an easy and enjoyable end-of-the-year show for parents or other classes.
- Get children to teach rhymes to their parents.

Rhymes

"How do I teach rhymes?"

- When you teach a rhyme to young children who have just started to learn English, do not expect their pronunciation to be clear or perfect. What they say at the beginning might be quite unintelligible, but they will quickly pick up the rhythm, stress and intonation. Their pronunciation will gradually correct itself as they learn to 'hear' the new sounds and, later, to distinguish the words.

- Try and keep your intonation consistent and natural.

- Do not separate words artificially, thinking your pupils will distinguish them more easily. e.g. not *One - two - put - on - my shoe* but *One - two - puton - my - shoe.*

- Recite the rhyme at normal speed.

- Always reinforce the meaning of the words with actions. ◆ SEE ACTIONS AND MIME PAGE 23

- Always use the same actions so children associate the words with the actions.

Example 1: 'One, two, Put on my shoe!'

'One, 'two,

'Put on my 'shoe!

'Three, 'four,

'Open the 'door!

'Five, 'six,

'Pick up 'sticks!

'Seven, 'eight,

'Don't be 'late!

'Nine, 'ten,

A 'big fat 'hen!

- T: *One* (put one finger in the air), *two* (put a second finger in the air), *Put on my shoe!* (Mime.)
  Exaggerate the rhythm and the actions. The children repeat the words and do the actions. Say the lines again, with the actions, and the children repeat them after you, with the actions.

- T: *Three* (hold three fingers up), *four* (four fingers up), *Open the door!* (Mime.)
  The children repeat the words and do the actions. Then say the lines again, with the actions, and the children repeat them after you, with the actions.

- Now say all four lines together, with the children repeating after you, and copying your actions:
  One, two,
  Put on my shoe! (The children repeat.)
  Three, four,
  Open the door! (The children repeat.)
  Add the next two lines:
  Five (hold five fingers up), *six* (six fingers up),
  Pick up sticks! (Mime.)
  The children repeat the words and do the actions. Say them again, with the actions, and the children repeat the words and do the actions again.

- Go back to the beginning of the rhyme and say it all again, as before.
- Leave the rhyme alone for a while, but come back to it later in the lesson. Children enjoy this break and change of activity, and it is less tedious for you!
- In the next lesson, add the rest of the rhyme.
- When the children are able to repeat the whole rhyme after you, with the actions, get them to perform it with you (rather than repeating it). As a final stage, do not say it at all, just do the actions to prompt the children.
- Once your pupils know the rhyme well, all you have to do is lift one finger in the air and then the other and they will automatically begin to recite it.
- You can also begin by:

   … asking the children to listen and watch while you recite and do the actions of the rhyme

   … then asking them to listen but do the actions with you

   … then following the procedure described above.

- Once the class knows the rhyme, divide them into two groups and give each group part of the rhyme to say. If you break a phrase up, be sure to do so naturally. e.g. lift one, and then two fingers up and point to group 1 who says *One, two*, then point to group 2, or do the action and point to group 2 who says *Put on my shoe!*

"What can I do if the children can´t hear the rhythm?"

If children have a problem hearing the rhythm:

… clap each stressed syllable while saying the phrase

… then get the children to clap the phrase while you say and clap it

… finally, get the children to clap and say the phrase with you.

Remember that in English the most important words in a sentence are stressed. This is why native English speakers seem to 'sing' when they are speaking.

Example 2: 'Jelly in the bowl'

ˈ*Jelly in the* ˈ*bowl,*

ˈ*Jelly in the* ˈ*bowl,*

ˈ*Wibble, wobble,*

ˈ*Wibble, wobble,*

ˈ*Jelly in the* ˈ*bowl,*

ˈ*Paper on the* ˈ*floor,*

ˈ*Paper on the* ˈ*floor,*

ˈ*Pick it up,*

ˈ*Pick it up,*

ˈ*Paper on the* ˈ*floor!*

When children like a rhyme or song, it is sometimes useful to extend it. This is better with short rhymes. *Jelly in the bowl* can be changed to *Cake on a plate, Eat it up* or *Water in a glass, Drink it up*, etc. Just keep the rhythm the same.

Try to memorise 'One, two, Put on my shoe!' or 'Jelly in the bowl' without clapping. Then add the claps. Do the claps make it easier to remember? (They should!) Then try teaching one of the rhymes to a class of beginners.

Here are some rhymes that are always popular with young children.

1 Three little monkeys

The rhyme with actions

'Three little 'monkeys, 'jumping on the 'bed, (Take three fingers and make them jump on the open palm of your other hand.)
'One fell 'off and 'broke his 'leg. (Take away one finger and clutch your leg.)
'Mother called the 'doctor and the 'doctor 'said: (Pretend you are phoning.)
'No more little 'monkeys, 'jumping on the 'bed!' (Shake your finger.)

'Two little 'monkeys, 'jumping on the 'bed,
'One fell 'off and 'broke his 'leg. (Take another finger away.)
'Mother called the 'doctor and the 'doctor 'said:
''No more little 'monkeys, 'jumping on the 'bed!'

'One little 'monkey, 'jumping on the 'bed,
'One fell 'off and 'broke his 'leg.
'Mother called the 'doctor and the 'doctor 'said:
''No more little 'monkeys, 'jumping on the 'bed!'

2 Baby's shoes

The rhyme with actions

'Baby's 'shoes,
'Sister's 'shoes,
'Brother's 'shoes,
'Mother's 'shoes,
'Father's 'shoes,
'GIANT'S 'shoes!

Hold your index fingers very close together, as though showing the size of something small. With each 'pair of shoes', increase the distance between your fingers until you spread your arms wide open for *Giant's shoes*.

Variation

Use the names of pupils from your class (e.g. *Bruno's shoes*) instead of names of family members, but always begin with *Baby's shoes* and finish with *Giant's shoes*.

3 Have you got a crocodile?

The rhyme with actions

'Have you 'got a 'croco'dile? (Put your arms straight out in front of you, with one palm above the other, like a crocodile's mouth. Clap your palms together on each stressed syllable.)

ˈNo, I ˈhaven't! ˈNo, I ˈhaven't! (Wag your finger in front of you, like a metronome, on the stressed syllables.)

ˈHave you ˈgot a ˈmonˈkey? (Put your hands under your armpits.)

ˈNo, I ˈhaven't! ˈNo, I ˈhaven't! (Wag your finger again.)

ˈHave you ˈgot a ˈblack ˈcat? (Put your cupped hands on your head, like a cat's ears.)

ˈYes, I ˈhave! ˈYes, I ˈhave! (Give a big clap on each *have* to show that it is shorter than *haven't*.)

Songs

TASK

What songs in English do you know? Do you like them? Why/Why not? Have they taught you anything about English? e.g. rhythm, vocabulary, etc.? Compare your answers with those of another teacher, if you can.

Why use music?

For the language teacher, songs have all the qualities of rhymes but develop the child's ear even more. Music helps children develop a sense of rhythm, which in turn helps them in such different areas as running and reading.

Playing an instrument, especially the guitar, will be a great asset to you as a teacher of young children. Virtually all children's songs can be played with just three chords and all you need to learn is a basic strum. Children are not a demanding audience and are fascinated by instruments of all types. Get them to sing a song and to accompany it on percussion instruments to help them hear the rhythm.

"How do I teach a song?"

- Teach a song like you teach a rhyme ◆ SEE PAGES 54–5, only beforehand, sing or play the whole song on the cassette recorder so the children can hear it in full. Ask them if they liked it.

- If the song has a chorus, teach this first. Then they can listen to the verses, which are more difficult, and sing the chorus. This makes them more attentive since they have to listen carefully to know when they have to join in.

- Sing (or play) a line and ask the children to be the 'echo' and sing the line back to you. When they have more or less learnt the line, add the next and then repeat from the beginning. Continue like this until the song is learnt.

- As always, remember to use actions, where possible.

- There are many cassettes with good music for young children (e.g. the *Wee Sing* series.)

- Tell the children you are going to record them singing and they will make a special effort. They will be delighted to listen to themselves.

Take a cassette recorder to your next lesson. Record your pupils singing. Make a note of their reactions before, and especially while, listening to the recording.

If you teach this song again, is there anything you could do differently? e.g. use pictures to teach key vocabulary, drill more, etc.?

Here are a few well-known songs , some with adapted versions for young children learning English! (If you do not know the music, just say the words rhythmically, like a rhyme.)

1 Head and shoulders

This traditional song is good for teaching parts of the body, especially if you change the last line.

The song with actions

'Head and 'shoulders, 'knees and 'toes, 'knees and 'toes,

'Head and 'shoulders, 'knees and 'toes, 'knees and 'toes,

And 'eyes, and 'ears, and 'mouth and 'nose,

'Head and 'shoulders, 'knees and 'toes, 'knees and 'toes.

Touch the part(s) of the body with both hands as you mention them.

Do the movements energetically, keeping the rhythm and your pupils will love it.

Variations

Add on other parts of the body as part of the song. e.g.:

'Bottom, 'bottom, 'bottom,

'Tummy, 'tummy, 'tummy.

In the next lesson, sing the original song, then the variation with *bottom* and *tummy* and then add on a new line:

'Hands, 'arms and legs!

'Hands, 'arms and legs!

2 Do you like soup?

This song is good for teaching *Do you like?* and *I like/I don't like.*

The song with actions

Do you like 'soup?

Do you like 'soup?

Do you like 'lots of 'soup? (Shake your hand as you say *lots of* to fix it in the children's memory.)

The children who like soup, sing:

'Yes! I like 'soup.

I like 'soup,

I like 'lots of 'soup!

The children who do not like soup, sing:

'No! I 'don't like 'soup! (They swing their arms vigorously on the word *don't*.)

I 'don't like 'soup!

I 'don't like 'lots of 'soup!

Variations

- Change *soup* to *salad, fish, spaghetti*, etc. or different categories.
- Change *like* to *want*.

3 Ten little Indians

This song is excellent for practising *has got* and the numbers 1–10. SEE PAGE 74 for how to use this as part of teaching *has got*.

The song with actions

It is fun if you get the children to sit cross-legged in a circle, like North American Indians.

'John has 'got (Cross your arms and bounce them slightly to the rhythm.)

'Ten (Uncross your arms, and hold up ten fingers.)

little (Hold your hands out, palms facing the floor.)

'Indians. (Hold your hands next to your head with the palms facing forwards and fingers sticking up like feathers.)

'John has 'got (Repeat actions.)

'Ten little 'Indians.

'John has 'got (Repeat actions.)

'Ten little 'Indians

'Ten little 'Indian 'boys. (On *boys*, cross your arms again.)

Once the children know this part, add the next.

Lift a finger for each number and put your palms out and facing the floor for the word *little*:

'One little, 'two little, 'three little 'Indians,

'Four little, 'five little, 'six little 'Indians,

'Seven little, 'eight little, 'nine little 'Indians,

'Ten little 'Indian 'boys. (On *Indian* put your fingers on top of your head like feathers; on *boys*, cross your arms.)

Variations

- Children love this song partly because they find it so difficult to coordinate the actions (adults sometimes have problems, too!).
- With the very young (three- and four-year-olds), you can get them just to cross their arms for *John has got* and then just add the action for *Indians*, for example.
- Sing the song slowly or quickly.
- Change *boys* to *girls*, *Indians* to *children*, etc.

Now, when you want to prompt or correct *has got*, all you have to do is cross your arms and slightly bounce them, and later just cross your arms.

4 Sally has got a red dress

This song is good for teaching *has got* and names for clothes and to start names for clothes and to start learning how to give personal descriptions. ◆ SEE PAGE 74 for how to use this as part of teaching *has got*.

The song

'Sally has 'got a 'red 'dress,
A 'red 'dress, a 'red 'dress,
'Sally has 'got a 'red 'dress,
To'day, to'day, to'day!

Variations

Red dress can be changed to other clothes, e.g. *blue jeans, pink shirt,* or, depending on the level of the group, to words for physical description, e.g. *long hair, brown eyes.*

5 Are you sleeping?

This traditional song is sung in many countries where it is known by different names (e.g. 'Frère Jacques', 'Pare Jaume', 'Bruder Jaque'). It is good for teaching the present continuous tense.

The song

'Are you 'sleeping? 'Are you 'sleeping,
'Brother 'John, 'Brother 'John?
'Morning bells are 'ringing,
'Morning bells are 'ringing,
'Ding, dang, 'dong,
'Ding, dang, 'dong.

Variations

Change the verbs to practise the present continuous. e.g.

'Are you 'sleeping? 'Are you 'sleeping?
'Yes, I 'am. 'Yes, I 'am.
'Come and put your 'clothes on,
'Come and put your 'clothes on,
'Right a'way,
'Right a'way!

'Are you 'washing? 'Are you 'washing?
'Yes, I 'am. 'Yes, I 'am.
'Come and have your 'breakfast,
'Come and have your 'breakfast,
'Right a'way,
'Right a'way!

'Are you 'eating? 'Are you 'eating?
'No, I'm 'not! 'No, I'm 'not!
'I am going to 'school, now.
'I am going to 'school, now.
'See you 'soon.
'See you 'soon!

6 London Bridge is falling down

This is another traditional action song that can be easily adapted for teaching *want* or *like* and numbers.

The song with actions

'London Bridge is 'falling down,
'Falling down, 'falling down.
'London Bridge is 'falling down,
My 'fair 'lady!

Basic procedure

- Form a bridge with a child by holding his hands up in the air. You can choose the child to do this with by using a 'dip'.  SEE PAGES 27–8
- Take the child to one side and together choose names for yourselves. e.g. one of you could be 'chocolate' and the other 'ice cream'. Do not tell the rest of the class what you have chosen.
- The other children get into a line and pass under the bridge as everybody sings.
- On the word *lady*, the people making the 'bridge' quickly bring down their arms and catch the child who is underneath. They sway him back and forth, counting from one to ten (or from 10 to 15, etc.). Then they ask the child e.g. *Do you like/want chocolate or ice cream?*
- The child answers and stands behind the member of the bridge whose name he has chosen. When there is a child behind each member of the bridge, they get together and form a new bridge. The line of children then have more than one bridge to run under, so the game does not take too long and the fun is multiplied.

Which of the above rhymes and songs would be useful to teach or reinforce these structures or word groups?

1	*has got*	5	the family
2	the present continuous	6	parts of the body
3	food	7	clothes
4	numbers	8	*like/want*

SEE KEY PAGE 91 for answers.

Drama

If you have been using actions to illustrate meaning, you have already begun to use drama in a very basic way. Here we look at how to introduce more advanced uses of drama, ones in which children interact with each other in different roles.

Cover the next section. Think of at least five reasons why drama is useful for teaching young children a language. Then check with the reasons given below.

Why use drama?

Drama is valuable in language teaching for the following reasons.

- When children are pretending to be someone else, especially if they are wearing a costume or a mask, they will very often lose their inhibitions and speak more freely.
- Acting stimulates children's imagination.
- Acting in a play means that they must learn a few lines by heart – or almost. Even if they have very few lines to say, the children have to repeat the words or sentences very often, so the particular words and structures become more assimilated.
- Saying their lines gives the children a chance to use English interactively in a context which is different from the classroom.
- Putting on a play for someone else gives the children's classroom activity a point. This sense of purpose stimulates them to make a special effort to learn.
- Putting on a play is fun and helps children learn to work together cooperatively.
- Acting in a play boosts children's self-esteem and can help shy children gain self-confidence.

Short poems

Short poems or sequences are ideal for as an introduction to more formal drama activities.

Basic procedure
- First teach the poem or sequence to the whole class, with the actions.
- Then divide the class into two groups, and give each group a part.
- Later, ask two children, or, at least, a smaller group, to perform it on their own.

Example: 'Rat-a-tat-tat!'

ˈRat-a-ˈtat-ˈtat! (Pretend to knock.)

ˈWho is ˈthat?

It's ˈgrandma's ˈpussycat! (Put your fingers around your eyes like glasses for grandma; cup your hand and put it behind you to represent a cat's tail.)

'What do you 'want?

A 'bowl of 'milk. (Cup your hands in front of you.)

'Where is your 'money? (Put both palms out, facing up for *where,* and rub your thumb and first two fingers for *money*.)

'In my 'pocket. (Put your hand in your pocket.)

'Where is your 'pocket? (This time pretend to put your hand in your pocket.)

'I for'got it! (Hit your forehead with your open palm.)

'Oh, you 'silly 'pussycat! (Shake your finger at the cat.)

- Explain to the children that this is the story of a cat who wants some milk. He goes to the dairy, knocks on the door and the milkmaid answers. The cat tells her that he has some money in his pocket, but everyone knows that cats don't have pockets! (Use the modern meaning of *pocket.* The original meaning in the rhyme is 'purse', but this does not matter. The idea is to make the children feel they like the cat, because he is so silly. They do!)
- Recite the poem and do the actions.

Sequences

One way of teaching the vocabulary necessary for an action story is to introduce it through a short 'sequence' of sentences accompanied by actions.

Example: for 'The enormous turnip'

- Put the children in pairs. Child A is the seed, and child B is the farmer.
- T: *The farmer plants the seed.* (Child A crouches into a ball while child B pretends to plant him.)
- T: *The farmer waters the seed.* (Child B does the action.)
- T: *The seed grows and grows and grows!* (Child A gradually stands up while the farmer follows him with his eyes.)
- T: *It's an almond tree!* (Child A stretches both arms wide out. Use any tree common to your region.)
- The children exchange roles.
- You may like to add a sequence with the farmer picking the fruit, putting it into the basket and eating it.

Invent a sequence for the farmer picking the fruit, putting it into the basket and eating it. ◆ SEE 'TAKE A CRAYON' PAGE 43. Compare your sequence with the one in the KEY PAGE 91.

End-of-the-year shows

Here are some ideas for for shows to put on at the end of the year.

Sketches

Perhaps the easiest 'play' to put on is simply a series of mini-dialogues (sketches), based on what you have taught the children during the year. e.g. two children (Rebeka and Daniel) pretend to meet in the middle of the class.

R: *Hello!*

D: *Hello! What's your name?*

R: *My name's Rebeka. What's your name?*

D: *My name's Daniel. How are you?*

R: *Fine, thank you. How are you?*

D: *Fine, thank you. Goodbye!*

R: *Goodbye!*

or

R: *I'm hungry! I'm hungry!*

D: *Do you want a hamburger?*

R: *No. I don't like hamburgers.*

D: *Do you want spaghetti?*

R: *I don't like spaghetti!*

D: *Oh, go away!*

Add a few songs and rhymes between the sketches, and you have a perfect show that also serves as a revision of what you have taught during the year.

Plays based on stories

With children whose English is at a higher level, you can make plays from well-known stories. Choose stories that:

… are simple

… are repetitive or accumulative, as most children's classics are. e.g. 'Goldilocks and the three bears', 'The three billy-goats Gruff', 'The enormous turnip', 'Little Red Riding Hood' (partly). (Storybooks for new readers like the Ladybird series are ideal for adapting into plays.)

… need very little change of scene. The fewer places the actors have to remember to go to, the better.

"How do I teach a play?"

The stages below describe how to teach a play based on a story.

Acting out the play

- Tell it as a story so the children know it well. ▶ SEE STORIES PAGES 43–5
- Act out the different parts of the play for the children. The first time, act out the whole play; the following times, leave out words and expressions and get the children to fill them in. (Do the action to prompt them.)
- You can also read or tell the story and get the pupils to do the actions as you go along.
- Finally, get the children to say the story while you do the actions.

- To stimulate your pupils, tell them you are going to put the play on for another class or, if you are lucky enough to have a video camera, that you are going to film it. Children love watching themselves on TV.

Preparing the play

- Have very few props and dress up the children as simply as possible.
- Use masks, cheap make-up or costume paints. Paint a child's nose and add whiskers to make him look like an animal, colour two red patches with lipstick on a child's cheeks for a girl (e.g. Goldilocks, Little Red Riding Hood). It does not matter what the children look like, as long as they feel the part, and children need very little to do this. At the same time, children are more likely to speak if disguised with a mask or make-up.
- Split certain roles between children to make them easier to learn and to allow more children participate. e.g. in 'Goldilocks and the three bears' have two Baby Bears and three Goldilockses.
- Choose small groups of friends to act together so that they give each other confidence. e.g. two friends are Mother and Father Bear, three friends are Goldilocks, etc.

Two short plays

The two short plays below show how you can start from a simple piece of drama and progress to a more complicated one. The first is all performed in one place, so there is no movement; the chorus does most of the speaking so the actual actors say very little. You may like to divide the role of narrator in each play between a number of groups, with each saying a particular line and all of them saying the last line.

1 The enormous turnip

If you have worked on this as a story, the narrators will more or less know their part before starting on the play. They should do the actions as they speak to help spectators understand what is going on. You could also have pictures of the different characters which some of the narrators can show as the characters come into the story.

Actors: A seed, the farmer, the wife, a boy, a girl, a dog, a cat and a mouse. The rest of the class is the narrator and stands in a group behind the actors.

N:	The farmer's got a seed. The farmer plants the seed. (*The farmer plants a seed, which is a child curled up very small on the floor.*)
N:	The farmer waters the seed. (*The farmer mimes.*) The seed grows and grows and grows. It is enormous! (*The seed gets bigger, little by little, so he is kneeling, with his hands on the floor.*) It's an enormous turnip!
N:	The farmer is hungry. He wants to eat the enormous turnip. He pulls and pulls. One, two, three! (*The farmer pulls the seed's waist.*) But he can't pull up the enormous turnip! (*The narrators shake their finger.*)
	The farmer calls the wife.
Farmer:	Wife, can you help me pull up the enormous turnip?

Wife :	OK. (*The wife puts her arms around the farmer's waist and helps to pull the seed.*)
N:	The wife pulls the farmer. They pull and they pull. One, two, three! But they can't pull up the enormous turnip. The wife calls the boy.
Wife:	Little boy, can you help me pull up the enormous turnip?
Little boy:	OK! (*He puts his arms around the wife's waist and everyone pulls the enormous turnip.*)
N:	The little boy pulls the wife, the wife pulls the farmer and the farmer pulls the enormous turnip. They pull and they pull. One, two, three! But they can't pull up the enormous turnip!
	(*The play continues with the boy calling the little girl, the little girl calling the dog, the dog calling the cat, and the cat calling the mouse.*)
Cat:	Can you help me pull up the enormous turnip?
Mouse:	Squeak! Squeak! OK!
N:	The mouse pulls the cat, the cat pulls the dog, the dog pulls the little girl, the little girl pulls the little boy, the little boy pulls the wife, the wife pulls the farmer and the farmer pulls the enormous turnip. They pull and they pull. One, two, three!
Everybody:	AND UP COMES THE ENORMOUS TURNIP! (*The seed jumps up. The whole line of actors fall down.*)

2 The four bears

This i s a proper play which is nevertheless very simple because it is based on only a few structures. It can be put on with six-year-olds in their second year of English with not too much work. It all depends how long you have had the children and what you have worked on with them.

It is a simple adaptation of 'Goldilocks and the three bears'. The main phrases used are: *Look! Look at, Let's, I (don't) like* and *I'm*. You will need to help the children during the play by prompting them with actions.

Props: A table and four cups/glasses. (This is the kitchen.) Four chairs. (This is the living room and the bedroom.)

Actors: Three Bad Girls (BG1, BG2, BG3), Father Bear, Mother Bear and two Baby Bears (FB, MB, BB1, BB2), Two pupils or the teacher play the narrator (N).

Stage directions: Put the table and chairs in separate parts of the 'stage' to indicate different rooms.

N:	Here are the four bears.
FB:	Hello! I'm Father Bear.
MB:	Hello! I'm Mother Bear.
BB1 and BB2 each say:	Hello! I'm Baby Bear.
N:	Mother Bear and Father Bear are in the kitchen.
MB calls:	Cocoa is on the table!
BB1:	Mmmm! I'm hungry!

BB2:	Mmmmm! I like cocoa! (*BBs go to kitchen.*)
BB1:	The cocoa is too hot!
BB2:	I don't like my cocoa!
MB:	Yes. The cocoa's too hot. Let's go to the forest. (*Bears go to the back of classroom and sit on the floor to watch. The three Bad Girls enter.*)
BG1:	Look! A house!
BG2:	Look! The door's open!
BG3:	I'm hungry!
N:	The three Bad Girls open the door. They go to the kitchen. (*BGs mime.*)
BG3:	Look! Cocoa! I like cocoa!
BG1 (*tastes FB's cocoa*):	I don't like this cocoa! It's too hot!
BG2 (*tastes MB's cocoa*):	I don't like this cocoa! It's too cold!
BG3 (*tastes BB1's cocoa*):	Mmmmm! I like this cocoa! (*BG1 and BG2 run and drink cocoa too. They finish it.*)
BG3:	I'm tired./Let's sit down./ I want to sit down.
N:	The three Bad Girls go to the living room.
BG1:	I don't like this chair. It's too hard. (*She pushes it away.*)
BG2:	I don't like this chair. It's too soft. (*She pushes it away.*)
BG3:	I like this chair! (*All BGs sit on a chair and turn it over, pretending to break it.*)
All BGs:	Look! The chair's broken!
BG3:	I'm tired./Let's sleep!/I want to sleep.
N:	The three Bad Girls go to the bedroom. (*BGs pretend to climb some stairs while T puts the four chairs upright again.*)
BG1 (*lies on chair*):	I don't like this bed. It's too hard!
BG2 (*lies on chair*):	I don't like this bed. It's too soft!
BG3 (*lies on chair*):	I like this bed! (*BG1 and BG2 run to chair and lie on it too.*)
All BGs:	Let's sleep!/I'm tired. (*They go to sleep. After a few seconds, they move off to the side of the stage. The teacher puts the chairs back in previous position, with one fallen down, as if broken.*)
N:	The four bears go to the house/go home.
MB:	Look! The door's open!
FB:	Let's go to the kitchen.
FB (*picks up his cup*):	Look! Look at my cocoa!
MB (*picks up her cup*):	Look! Look at my cocoa!
BB1:	Look! My cocoa is all gone! (*Cries.*)

MB:	Let's go to the living room. (*Bears move over to the four chairs.*)
FB (*goes to his chair*):	Look! Look at my chair!
MB (*goes to her chair*):	Look! Look at my chair!
BB2:	Look! My chair is broken! (*Cries, and MB consoles him.*)
FB:	Let's go to the bedroom! (*Bears pretend to walk upstairs. Teacher replaces chairs, and BGs come and lie on one, as before.*)
FB:	Look! Look at my bed!
MB:	Look! Look at my bed!
BB1:	Look! The bad girls are in my bed!
BGs (*wake up and shout*):	The four bears! Help! Help! (*BGs run off stage and bears run after them.*)
N:	And the three Bad Girls never went to the forest again.

Actors and narrators go to the front of the class, bow and say:

I was a narrator, I was Father Bear, etc. *and everybody claps.*

CHAPTER 8

Teaching some basic structures

This chapter aims to give you some ideas as to how, over a period of time, you can teach young children some basic structures in English. Young children have no notion of grammar (nor do they need it), but learn through imitation, intuition and lots of practice. Therefore it is **not** suggested that in one lesson you focus **exclusively** on one structure, but rather that you use activities suggested for different structures. Each activity should be repeated and augmented in following lessons until the children have learnt the structure to your satisfaction. Then, as children learn as quickly as they forget, you will need to repeat the activities now and again in subsequent lessons.

Most of the activities here are very short and should only last a few minutes each. Exceptions are the games, follow-up and 'final focus' activities.

The three structures selected are: *can* for asking permission, the present tense of the verb *to be* and the verb *have/has got*. Children are basically egocentric and their main interest is themselves and their possessions, thus the importance of the verbs *be* and *have*, which are also of course basic concepts in any language. Children need to learn to ask permission as an essential part of their socialisation. Getting them to do this also helps to create an atmosphere where English is spoken, right from the beginning.

Can for asking permission

Aim

To teach pupils to use *Can I ... ?* to ask for permission in a variety of contexts.

1 Back-chaining

A technique called BACK-CHAINING can be used to introduce *can* for asking permission.

Basic procedure
- Offer the children something they like such as a sweet, a sticker, etc. and explain in L1 what you are going to do. e.g. *We are going to learn how to ask for a sweet.*
- Start with the last word in the question, and build the question up backwards.

  T: *please?*

  Get children to repeat *please?*

  Repeat the word using different voices (e.g. a whisper, a shout, a high/low voice, a squeaky one).

  When the children can say *please?*, say the preceding word (*sweet*). After repeating *sweet* a few times, add *please* (*sweet, please?*) and continue like this with the rest of the question.

  ¹please?

  ¹sweet, ¹please?

  a ¹sweet, ¹please?

ʹhave a ʹsweet, ʹplease?

ʹI have a ʹsweet, ʹplease?

ʹCan I have a ʹsweet, ʹplease?

- Remember to keep a steady rhythm and consistent intonation. The whole process should only take three or four minutes at the most.

- Later in the lesson, repeat it. In the following lesson, most children will only have remembered *sweet, please?* but in no time, they will be using the whole question.

- If you are not used to using BACK-CHAINING, practise in front of a mirror, reading the sentence from a piece of paper. It is worth learning to BACK-CHAIN as it is such an easy way to teach children a long sentence or difficult structure.

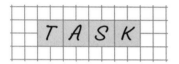

Think of a question that your pupils need in class and teach it to them next lesson by BACK-CHAINING.

2 Asking in class

Now, start using *can* for permission in class. When children need pencils, for example, before you give one to a child say *Can I have a pencil, please?* Get each child to ask this before you give him the pencil. Use the same rhythm as when you taught the class to ask for a sweet. Little by little, your children will get the idea and start substituting *pencil, crayon,* etc. for *sweet.*

Variations

Later, start adding adjectives, e.g. *Can I have a red pencil, please?*

Then change the verb: *Can I go to the toilet, please?*

3 Follow-up: drawing in a group

When the children know the words for the colours, this is a good activity to practise *Can I ...?*

Basic procedure

- Put the children in groups of about four or five and give each child a crayon of a different colour.

- Ask them to draw a picture. In order to complete their picture, they have to ask the others in their group: *Can I have the yellow, please?* Teach them to answer *Yes, here* and give their crayon to their friend.

Variation

To make the activity more interesting, give out different colours of Plasticine and get the children to make a picture with it on a piece of black card.

Reinforcement

Go out and play 'Crocodile'. SEE PAGE 31

4 Follow-up: shopping

Later on, you can get the children to pretend they are shopping so that they learn to use *can* in a different, yet realistic situation. If they are learning words for food, set up a grocer's or greengrocer's. Alternatively, you could set up a stationer's that sells things for school, or a clothes shop.

- Use basic structures. At first, play the role of the shopkeeper. Here is a sample conversation.

Shopkeeper: *Good morning. (Can I help you?)*
Customer: *Good morning. Have you got apples?*
S: *Yes. I've got green apples and red apples.*
C: *Can I have green apples, please?*
S: *How many apples (do you want)?*
C: *I want/Can I have three apples?*
S: *Here.*
C: *How much is it?*
S: *Five (francs).*
C: *One, two, three, four, five. (Customer taps shopkeeper's open palm five times.)*
S: (gives apples to B): *Here.*
C: *Thank you.*
S: *Goodbye!*
C: *Goodbye!*

- Later, you can have more than one shop with various pupils playing shopkeeper.

  Variation

  If you are feeling adventurous, you can even organise a sort of flea market in the class where the children bring in some old toys to sell among themselves. Set a maximum price for each item which is low. Each child has a stall (a chair) which he can open or close depending on whether he is buying or selling. You might like to ask a few parents in to help.

General practice

- Insist right from the beginning that your pupils use *please* and *thank you*, which are very important when speaking English and may be used more regularly than in other cultures.

- Once your pupils can more or less ask permission with *can*, be firm. Don't let them get away with asking in L1 because this will soon become a habit and some children will test you constantly by doing so.

The verb *to be* in the present tense

Aim

To teach the positive and negative forms of the verb *to be* in the present tense.

1 *I am*

Basic procedure

- Pat your chest twice and say *I* (pat) *am* (pat) ... *intelligent!* (Make a sign for this, e.g. put your finger to your temple and take it out to the side.) *I* (pat) *am* (pat) ... *strong!* (Use a deep voice and flex your arm muscles.)

- It is essential to use actions to communicate your meaning. ◆ SEE ACTIONS AND MIME PAGE 23

- Always exaggerate your actions. Choose adjectives that make children feel good about themselves, so that they will assimilate them naturally – they all want to feel intelligent, strong, pretty, etc.

- In subsequent lessons, add useful adjectives. e.g. *hungry, clean, small, big, dirty, tired, angry, hot, cold, ill, nice.*

- Because English uses *to be* + an adjective to express concepts that in many languages are expressed with the equivalent of *to have* + a noun (e.g. *I am hungry: Ich habe hunger, J'ai faim, tinc fam, tengo hambre*), teach those adjectives straight away so that the children associate them naturally with *to be*. This is especially important as older children, when they begin to learn to write, start translating what they are not absolutely sure of. ◆ SEE WHAT HAPPENS WHEN CHILDREN BEGIN TO WRITE? PAGE 74

Contracted forms

Immediately after using the full form of the verb (e.g. *I am strong*) repeat the phrase using the contracted form (*I'm strong*). If you also use the contracted form when speaking, children will gradually start using it themselves. This is true for any contraction.

2 *You are* – 'hypnotising' your class

You have probably used *you are* in games and in your instructions to the pupils, so they have heard it before and it will ring a bell with them, at least. Now you can teach it by 'hypnotising' them!

Basic procedure

- Say in a theatrical voice *I'm going to hypnotise you! Ready? ... Sleep! ... Sleep!* The children put their heads on their desks and mime being asleep. (They keep their eyes open though!)

- Say *You are big, big, BIG!* Mime the adjective and use voice inflection to emphasise the meaning. The children mime with you. (Gradually over the following lessons, drop the actions and use only voice inflection and finally, only say the words. e.g. *You are fat, fat, FAT!* The children continue to mime.)

- When you have finished, say *You are going to wake up. Ready? Wake up!* Everybody 'wakes up' and you put a look of surprise on your face: *Oh! What happened?*

- Later, start mixing words that sound alike (*hungry/angry*) to teach them to listen and discriminate.

- This activity can be used when your class is overexcited and you need to calm them down. ◆ SEE PAGE 16

3 *It is*

It is simply taught through showing pictures of singular objects that are important in children's lives (e.g. *ball, house, cat*) and should be taught within a sentence. e.g. *It is a ball*. For an explanation of why you should use full sentences ◆ SEE PAGE 21. There is absolutely no need to explain that *it* is used for objects – just let the children use it automatically.

4 *They are/We are*

- Later, you can start showing pictures of plural objects. Start with objects that the children already know in the singular. This will familiarise them with *they are* used with objects (they will already be quite familiar with the words as you will have certainly used them in class). For children aged five and older, you can mention that *they are* is for 'more than one'.

- *We are* comes naturally through use: help your pupils to acquire the notion by drawing a circle in front of you with your hand every time you use it. The circle will give the idea of *we are* as encompassing you and the class.

5 He/she is

When teaching *he* and *she*, you can tell the class that girls are silent because you say *shhhh* (put your finger to your lips) ... *shhhhee!* for girls. It's an easy way to help pupils distinguish between *he* and *she* and at the same time, helps work on the /sh/ sound, which is difficult for certain non-English speakers to pronounce.

Basic procedure

- Point to a boy and say *He is intelligent!*
- Point to another boy and say *He is strong!*
- Point to a girl, with your finger on your lips and say *Shhhe is pretty!*
- Point to another girl and say *She is strong!*

Do the actions while speaking.

- Then revert to a drawing or picture and say *He is fat!* etc.
- Show another picture of a person and elicit the sentence.
- Finally, ask each child to say something about the classmate beside him (help by doing an action, if the child needs it).

By first using a classmate and then a picture, you are making *he/she* a general concept: *he* is not used just for your friend, but any male person, child or adult.

6 The negative

Basic procedure

- Choose a slim (not a skinny!) child and say *He is fat!*
- Then act as though you have made a big mistake (remember to exaggerate to make more impact and and get more attention) and add with a smile *No! He is NOT fat.* When you say *not*, slap one hand on the other loudly.
- Then say normally *He isn't fat.*

The slap you use on *not*:

... makes an action game out of the negative, which is fun

... adds sound and rhythm that stay with the child, telling him internally when to place the *not*

... can be used to remind children to add the *not* when they are trying to use the negative, or to correct them if they have forgotten to use it.

7 Final focus

Basic procedure

- When you feel your children have assimilated these forms of the verb *to be* (remember that in the meantime they will have learnt other structures), give them a picture to colour which shows a number of people who are different shapes and who have different expressions that they can describe (*small, big, fat, thin, cold, angry*, etc.). It should also include some of the objects you have taught so that they can talk about them using *it* and *they*. ◆ SEE PHOTOCOPIABLE PAGE 12
- If you do not have suitable pictures for them to colour, ask them to find pictures in a magazine, cut them out and glue them on a sheet of paper.
- While the children are colouring or sticking pictures onto paper, go around and ask them to talk about their picture(s). Point to the different people or things and get the children to make sentences about them.
- Assess what each child has assimilated and make a note of this in his notebook. Get each child, when he has finished, to stick the picture(s) in his notebook.
- Reward each child by drawing a smiley face on his sheet. ◆ SEE GIVING REWARDS PAGE 15

"Why do I need a final focus activity?"

T A S K

Cover the next section. Think of at least three benefits of a final focus activity as described above. Then compare your list with the one below.

This kind of activity is helpful in the following ways.
- It gives you and the children a summary of what you have done.
- It provides you with assessments of each individual's progress.
- It shows parents what their children are learning.
- The children have the satisfaction of seeing something concrete that shows that they have 'passed a level'.
- If you put the picture(s) in a book, you:
… will give the children a lot of pleasure as they love books of their own work
… will create a sort of picture dictionary that you and the children can refer back to.

"What happens when children begin to write?"

When children begin to write, you may be surprised to find that many children start to translate from L1 instead of writing down what they would normally say, making a lot of typical grammar mistakes. This is because writing is a slower process than speaking, so children begin to think about what they are writing and refer back to L1, forgetting the language they have already acquired in a more automatic way. Typically, if you ask them their age, they will answer *I am eight*, and then write *I have eight*. Teachers have to work on teaching their pupils to listen to their intuition and not their intellect. Likewise, it is important that teachers teach their pupils to be mentally 'agile', in other words, to find ways of expressing themselves when they do not know the right word or structure. e.g. saying *the door isn't open* if they do not know the word *closed*.

Have/has got

Aim

To teach the forms *he/she has got, have you got …?, Yes, I have, No, I haven't.*

1 Song: 'Ten Little Indians'

- It is always a good idea to use a verb or structure before you actually teach it so that the children are already familiar with it. So with *has got*, you can start by teaching the action song 'Ten little Indians'. ◆ SEE PAGE 59
- The action of crossing their arms when they sing *has got* can then become your prompt for using this form of the verb, or correcting them when they use something else instead (*have got* or *is are* most common mistakes).

2 Song: 'Sally has got a red dress'

- Now add the well-known children's song 'Sally has got a red dress' to teach the meaning of *has got* and to start working on personal description. ◆ SEE PAGE 60 If you don't know the tune, use the words as a chant, with the rhythm shown.

Basic procedure

- Ask a child to come to the front of the class. Say *Rebeka, come here, please. Oh, look! Rebeka has got blue jeans!* Hold her hands and swing them back and forth, saying or chanting:
  Re'beka has got 'blue 'jeans,
  'Blue 'jeans, 'blue 'jeans!
  Re'beka has got 'blue 'jeans,
  To'day, to'day, to'day!
  Sit down, Rebeka. Angie, come here! Oh! What has Angie got? Angie has got a green sweater! (sing song)

- Get the children to sit in a circle and put their arms around each other's necks or waists and sway with the music from side to side. This just adds that element of fun to a song that maybe the children don't feel like singing that day.

3 Rhyme: 'Have you got a crocodile?'

This rhyme teaches them the question form *have you got* and the short answers *No, I haven't* and *Yes, I have*. ◈ SEE PAGE 56 for the words and actions.

Basic procedure

- Give a big clap on *have*, so the children are aware of the shortness of *have* as compared to *haven't* since they tend to confuse these.

- Now, all you have to do is to ask a child a new question but using the rhythm and intonation of the rhyme. Use vocabulary that they already know, preferably something that they are wearing or have got in front of them so you can point at it while asking e.g. *Have you 'got a 'sweater?*

- Finally, get the children to start making their own questions.

4 Game: 'Memory'

When the children have assimilated the forms above, reinforce them by playing 'Memory'. ◈ SEE PAGE 49

5 Follow-up: *has* and *is*

While you have been teaching *have/has got*, you will probably have also been working on *he/she is*. Your pupils will need a lot of practice before they begin using *is* and *has* without confusing them. Here is a good activity to help them start seeing the difference in meaning between them.

- Ask a child to come to the front of the class and stand on a chair so everyone can see him. Say *Martin is strong! He is intelligent! He has got a red sweater. He has got blue jeans*. At the beginning, only use vocabulary that the children know. Later you can add other useful vocabulary for very simple descriptions.

- A good game to continue this work of distinguishing *is* and *has* and of learning to describe people is 'Thumbs up!'. ◈ SEE PAGE 35

6 Final focus

A picture dictation ◈ SEE PAGE 45 is one way to complete work on this structure, or one form of it.

- The children simply listen carefully and draw what you tell them.

- This activity should get more and more complicated throughout the school year so as to develop children's listening and comprehension abilities.

```
T A S K
```

Which other activities in Chapters 5–7 can help you reinforce *can* for asking permission, the verbs *to be* and *have/has got*? Look back at these chapters to find out.

Taking an overview

Teaching a language is very like making a jelly: you add the ingredients gradually, it thickens while you stir it, and it only gels much later!

When you are teaching a language to children, you introduce little bits of new language at a time, repeating what you have taught very often, with love and patience. At first the language is like a rainfall of meaningless sounds to the children – and there are sounds that they often cannot even hear because they do not exist in their mother tongue. Little by little, they learn to hear these new sounds, to distinguish words, to give them meaning, to reproduce them to make sentences like yours, in the right context, and finally to create their own sentences! At the same time they are learning that an object has not just one, but many names (e.g. *dog, perro, chien*) and that different languages work differently (e.g. word order, gender).

At this point, it is very important that they hear as much English, and of as wide a variety, as possible. If you can, use tapes, videos and storybooks. (You can buy many cheaply second-hand.) If you know any English people, invite them to your class to tell them a story or just to talk to them. Exchange materials with other teachers and find out what works with their classes. (As well as materials, share ideas and experiences with other teachers. It is very helpful and stimulating to discuss your difficulties or exciting teaching experiences with others.)

If you are aware of the difficulties your pupils may have with the language, you may, at first, be afraid to use too much of it with your pupils. Don't be! Work on the language you are teaching, but at the same time use English as much as you can to give the pupils as much passive language as possible. You will see the fruits of this later.

It is worth keeping a record of your lessons, noting down what worked well and can be used again, and what did not work so well. Here are some reasons why an activity may not have worked.

- The children were not properly prepared for the activity.
- You spent too much time setting it up and the children lost interest.
- The children did not understand what they had to do. (Did you break the activity down into enough steps?)
- The activity expected too much from them.
- It was too long or too complicated.
- The activity was not suitable for their age or tastes (e.g. it was too difficult, or too babyish).
- The children simply did not find it stimulating, or did not like it (e.g. a song).
- You did not give them the activity at an appropriate time of day.

Ask yourself: 'Can I remodel the activity and try it again?' Remember that although an activity that really works well almost always works well, some activities work better with one class than with another, and children often have to get used to an activity to enjoy it. Classes that have a majority of boys often need more physical action than those with a majority of girls who want to sit and 'work' more frequently. Be sensitive to the character and mood of your class.

And lastly, as we said in an earlier chapter, it really does not matter how much English you know. If your pupils love you, and young children are very ready to do so, they will learn from you.

1 Classroom language 1

Class management

Come here.

Go back.

Stand up.

Sit down.

Sit cross-legged on the floor.

Sit with your legs out.

Sit with your legs wide apart.

Get into line.

Make a line/circle.

Hold hands.

Cross/Uncross your arms/legs.

Lie on your mat.

Hands up/down.

Be quiet.

Calm down.

Whisper.

Shout.

Speak quietly.

Repeat after me.

Put away your things.

Put it/the ... back.

Put ... in the bin.

Clean up./Tidy up.

Can you lend me your ..., please?

Give out the ... .

Pull up/down the blinds.

Turn on/off the tap. (US = faucet)

Flush the toilet.

Tie up/Untie your shoes.

Do up/Undo your jacket.

Wipe your nose.

Blow your nose.

a hanky/a tissue

Classroom materials

a sheet of paper

card (US = bristol board)

Plasticine

chalk

crayons; to crayon

felt tips (US = magic markers)

oil pastels

coloured pencils

paints; to paint

paint brushes

a rubber

Rub out the ... .

tape/sellotape (US = scotch tape); to tape

masking tape

glue; to glue

a drawing pin (US = thumb tack)

a pin

a safety pin

Pin the ... up on the wall.

a stapler;/staples; to staple

a paper punch

string

Fold the ... in half.

Stick the ... to the ... .

Cut out the shape.

Tie/Untie a knot.

Action games

the playground

the gym

the basketball court

the football pitch

the water fountain

a bench

Make two groups.

Stand in the middle.

Don't cross the line.

Stay behind the line.

Sit on the ground.

Stand side by side.

Stand face to face.

Stand back to back.

Skip.

Hop.

Take two (giant/small) steps.

Freeze!

You're it.

You're out.

It's not fair.

Cheat!

It's my/your/his turn.

We won/The winners are … .

We lost/The losers are … .

It's a draw.

Board games

the board

a square

a counter/a man

Roll the dice.

Go forward/back two squares.

Miss a turn.

It's your turn again.

Card games

a pack of cards

Shuffle the cards.

Deal (out) the cards.

Turn over a card.

Put the card face down/up.

Songs

the first /second verse

the first/last line

the chorus

Everybody join in!

3 Body puzzle for 'Beetle'

SEE PAGE 37

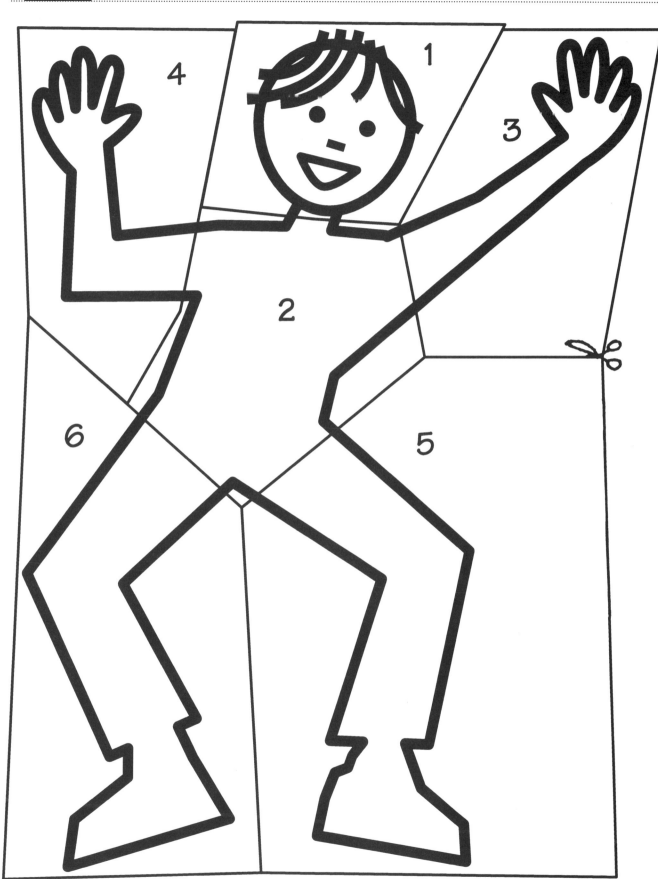

Teaching Very Young Children, © Genevieve Roth, 1998

SEE PAGE 37

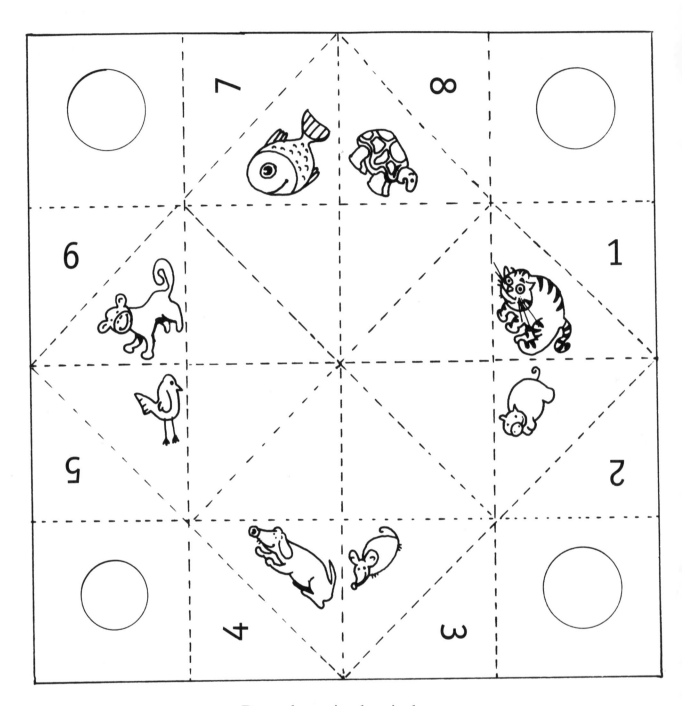

Put colours in the circles.

Teaching Very Young Children, © Genevieve Roth, 1998

5 The Park 1

Teaching Very Young Children, © Genevieve Roth, 1998

SEE PAGE 40

SEE PAGE 47

Teaching Very Young Children, © Genevieve Roth, 1998

 **11** Grid

SEE PAGE 50

1	2	3
4	5	6
7	8	9
10	11	12

SEE PAGE 73

Teaching Very Young Children, © Genevieve Roth, 1998 **PHOTOCOPIABLE**

Glossary

BACK-CHAINING	Teaching a whole expression as a chant by starting at the end and finishing at the beginning. It is the opposite of front-chaining.
FLASHCARDS	Large cards with pictures and/or words for use in the classroom, either by the teacher, e.g. for drills, or by pupils, e.g. in games.
PROJECT CENTRE	A space or corner in the classroom where the children work on specific long-term projects. All the material related to the project, such as reference books, project notebooks, etc, is kept there for the children to use.
REALIA	Real things which you bring into the classroom to use as a teaching aid. e.g. real apples and pears, rather than pictures, to teach the names of fruit.

Further reading

Brewster, J, Ellis, G and Girard, D *The Primary English Teacher's Guide*
Penguin, 1991
A valuable guide to teaching techniques and learning strategies for language acquisition at primary level, with many practical suggestions and lists of resources.

Brumfit, C, Moon, J and Tongue, R *Teaching English to Children: from Practice to Principle* Addison Wesley Longman, 1991
A thorough introduction to the background theory and practice of primary EFL. An essential for every EFL library.

Cant, A and Superfine, W *Developing Resources for Primary* Richmond Publishing, 1997
A collection of resource, activities, games, etc. for the primary English classroom, all presented in such a way that teachers can transfer the ideas to other topics of language in the classroom.

House, S *An Introduction to Teaching English to Children* Richmond Publishing, 1997
A thorough introduction covering the basics of teaching EFL to children, with a variety of simple activities.

Reilly, V and Ward, S *Very Young Learners* OUP, 1997
This contains ideas and advice for teaching very young learners. It includes a wide variety of activities using games, songs, drama, stories and art and craft.

Vale, D with Feunteun, A *Teaching Children English* CUP, 1995
This deals with different aspects of methodology and classroom practice. It includes stories, rhymes, songs, practical tasks and language tasks.

Wright, A *Storytelling with Children* OUP, 1996
There are many practical ideas in this book which can be used by both inexperienced and experienced primary EFL teachers. It is an excellent resource for traditional stories and stories which can be created by the children themselves.

Key

Chapter 3, page 20

Improvements: More fluent. More mistakes than last time, but language is richer. Isabel's English is progressing well.

A/the much better.

Problems: Uses *-ing* verbs and *going to* with certain ease but still mixes them up (normal)

General: Excellent

Chapter 5, page 38

1   colours: Touch something, Thumbs up!, Snapdragon
2   parts of the body: Writing on backs, Beetle
3   numbers: The number game, How many fingers …?, Writing on backs
4   action verbs: Run, run!, Go to … , Crocodile
5   clothes: Touch something, Thumbs up!
6   places: Go to …, Crocodile, The number game
7   classroom objects: Touch something
8   possession: It's your ball, Thumbs up!, Beetle, Snapdragon
9   *to be*: Thumbs up!, Snapdragon
10 permission: Crocodile
11 *Whose … ?*: Whose is it?
12 *there is/there are*: There are three in your group, How many fingers …?
13 *How many …?*: How many fingers …?

Chapter 6, page 40

Suggested answers

pen, pencil, felt tip: *pen* is easy, use it to teach *pencil*. Visually a *felt tip* is long and thin and writes like a pen and pencil so children will remember it more easily if you put it into the same category.

ruler, rubber: both begin with *r*. Teach the shorter word first.

sharpener: difficult. Clap out the rhythm and/or follow the sound with your finger.

glue: use word association through rhyme. Say *blue glue* and hold your nose while speaking, as though you are going underwater.

Chapter 6, page 52

1 colours: Who has …?, Show me, Grids

2 parts of the body: Grids, In my bag there is …

3 clothes: Who has …?, Bingo

4 action verbs: Bingo, Memory

5 classroom objects: Spin, What's in the bag …?, Kim's game

6 rooms of the house and furniture: Spin, Yes and no chairs

7 places: Who has …?, Bingo

8 animals: Who has …?, Bingo, Yes and no chairs, Kim's game, In my bag there is …

Chapter 7, page 61

1 *has got*: Ten little Indians, Sally has got a red dress

2 the present continuous: Are you sleeping?, London Bridge is falling down

3 food: Do you like soup?

4 numbers: Ten little Indians, London Bridge is falling down

5 the family: Baby's shoes

6 parts of the body: Head and shoulders

7 clothes: Sally has got a red dress

8 *like/want*: Do you like soup?, London Bridge is falling down

Chapter 7, page 63

The farmer picks the fruit (the apples, the cherries, etc.).
The farmer puts the fruit (the apples, the cherries) in his basket.
The farmer eats the fruit (the apples, the cherries).
It's/They're delicious!

Index of activities and language

(the numbers in brackets refer to photocopiable pages)

Index of topics

(the numbers in brackets refer to photocopiable pages)